BEHOLD
THE
CHRIST

BEHOLD THE CHRIST

Roland H. Bainton

Assisted by Sumathi Devasahayam

A COLLINS ASSOCIATES BOOK

Harper & Row, Publishers
New York, Hagerstown, San Francisco, London

First Harper & Row paperback published in 1976.

ISBN: 0-06-060353-4

LIBRARY OF CONGRESS CATALOG CARD NUMBER: 73-18678

ACKNOWLEDGEMENTS

Many of the works from which selections herein are taken are protected by copyright, and may not be reproduced in any form without the consent of the authors, their publishers, or their agents. Every effort has been made to trace the ownership of all selections in this book and to obtain the necessary authorization for their use. If any errors or omissions have occurred in this regard, corrections will be made in all future editions of the book.

Biblical texts generally taken from the REVISED STANDARD VERSION of the Bible, © 1946, 1952 by the Division of Christian Education, National Council of Churches.

I wish to express my gratitude to Patricia Collins for the design and layout of the book, to Susan Berkowitz for indefatigable editorial labors, and to Daniel Ossorio and David Richarda of Yale University for the photographic representations.

Roland H. Bainton,
New Haven, Conn.

To Christopher Peck

PREFACE

This work is not directed primarily toward art historians incidentally interested in religion, but to persons religiously experienced, who find in art clues to a deeper understanding and a means of commending to others their faith. Consequently, details important for art historians will be passed over lightly. There is, for example, a history of depictions of the crucifixion which includes sketches, century by century, of the prevailing types. The main differences have to do with the length of the apron serving as a loincloth. Did it end above the knee, on the knee, or under the knee? Such information may serve to fix the place and time; but for religion all this is trivial. The case is different with respect to what Jesus as judge was seen sitting on. Was it a throne, the circle of the earth, or a rainbow? The degree of elevation had a bearing on his role.

Religious art must be focused on the subject rather than on the manner of depiction, unless the manner reveals something significant in the attitude of the artist to the subject. Sometimes an artist is obsessed by the manner to the neglect of the subject. He may have just discovered new skills in composition, color combinations, perspective, and the like; to exhibit his competence one subject is as good as another. If the subject is religious the treatment is not.

Then what marks a work of art as something religious and not merely an exercise in style? A deeper question is whether art can be religious at all. Is it possible to make the invisible visible, to depict that which "eye hath not seen"? Must religion be expressed in words rather than in pictures? These questions will engage the Introduction.

A theme running throughout this book is the interplay of Christianity and the social scene as exhibited in art. Every generation has selected from the body of material about Jesus that which has spoken to its condition. Why was it that not until the fourteenth century do we find a picture of "a decree went out from Caesar Augustus"? Why was there no illustration of the words, "There was no room for them in the inn" until the sixteenth century? Why was Christ shown for a thousand years as alive on the cross and thereafter for centuries as dead? Actual situations give answers and this is the point at which a church historian may have something to offer to the historian of art.

A related point is that every land and time has transported Palestine to its own locale. In the fourteenth century, the Jewish men in the gospels were depicted wearing the hats at that time worn in the ghetto. A modern American Indian shows the Wise Men arriving in canoes. In Ghana, Joseph, Mary, and the Babe are black. This process of adaptation is inevitable—sometimes enriching, sometimes impoverishing, sometimes perverting. Christianity cannot spread without translations into the languages and cultural modes of a people. The process may mean the Christianizing of paganism or the paganizing of Christianity.

Then, of course, comes the question of the norm by which one decides. Answers involve value judgments arising from one's view as to the essential nature of Christianity. Personal opinions cannot be avoided. I have not hesitated to express my own, nor to bestow praise and blame. Many will dissent. By the sharing of judgments sounder judgments are achieved.

The scope of this work is formidable and I have wondered whether I dare enter where angels fear. But there is no way to overcome fragmentation save by attempts at synthesis. Broad generalizations are precarious but those who refuse to venture may bog down in trivia.

The procedure after the introduction is to take up episodes in the life of Christ, though not all are covered for lack of space. The main stress is on the themes that have been most abundantly illustrated because they are connected with the great festivals of the Christian year: Christmas, Good Friday, and Easter— the nativity, the passion, and the resurrection. But even in the nativity cycle there are omissions of the annunciation, the visitation, and the presentation. Between the nativity and the passion only some attention is given to miracles and parables. Within the episodes, the treatment is roughly chronological, though sometimes there are vast leaps in order to contrast types. An effort has been made to give examples not only from all periods, but from many places, including the lands of the younger churches in modern times.

CONTENTS

INTRODUCTION 13

1. NATIVITY 34
2. SHEPHERDS 46
3. WISE MEN 52
4. SLAUGHTER OF THE INNOCENTS 66
5. FLIGHT INTO EGYPT 70
6. BOYHOOD AT NAZARETH 74
7. BAPTISM 78
8. MIRACLES 84
9. PARABLES 88
10. TRIUMPHAL ENTRY 94
11. ANOINTING AT BETHANY 98
12. CLEANSING OF THE TEMPLE 102
13. WASHING THE DISCIPLES' FEET 106
14. LAST SUPPER 110
15. GETHSEMANE 120

16.	ARREST	124
17.	PETER'S DENIAL	128
18.	TRIALS	132
19.	CRUCIFIXION	144
20.	DEPOSITION FROM THE CROSS AND PIETÀ	158
21.	RESURRECTION	164
22.	CHRIST BEYOND HISTORY	189
23.	VINE	190
24.	LAMB	194
25.	BRIDEGROOM	198
26.	SECOND PERSON OF THE TRINITY	202
27.	PANTOCRATOR	206
28.	JUDGE	210
	EPILOGUE	215
	List of Illustrations and Bibliography	218

Figure 1. Derick Baegert.
Luke paints the Virgin and Child

INTRODUCTION

NE DOES NOT KNOW how Jesus looked. No authentic likeness has come down to us. The New Testament gives us scarcely a hint. The early Christian writers did see in Jesus a fulfillment of the "suffering servant" of whom the prophet Isaiah said, "he has no form or comeliness . . . and no beauty that we should desire him." The stress was not, however, on this verse, but on the one that followed: "and the Lord has laid on him the iniquity of us all . . . and with his stripes we are healed."

The writers of the New Testament were interested in what Jesus said and did rather than in how he looked. Perhaps this is all to the good, because it means that each period and people has been free to envision him in its own way. The diverse pictures are not false. Each has seized upon some valid feature. The variety attests to

Figure 2. Martin Schongauer. Veronica's napkin

Christ's universality. However, there may also be distortions, and any depiction which excludes the others is to that degree false. The purpose of this book is to describe and evaluate the varieties. The procedure is to deal with successive episodes in the life of Christ, and then with the Christ above history.

Those who knew Jesus after the flesh had no need of pictures, and those who came after transmitted no descriptions. But successors did wish to know. The common people in particular desired a visible image, and it was they who initiated the impetus in Christian art. Leaders, like the theologian Paul, were determined to know Christ no longer after the flesh. The common folk were not enthralled by a gospel so ethereal, however.

During the centuries, legends as to his appearance accumulated. The biographer of Constantine, Eusebius, told of a statue of a woman kneeling in supplication before a man with outstretched hands. She was the woman with the issue of blood. Her name was Berenike. The man was, of course, Jesus.

One legend claimed that Abgar, the king of Edessa, had sent a messenger to Jesus who returned with a portrait. And according to another legend, the evangelist Luke was alleged to have painted the Virgin Mary and the babe. We even have a picture of him at his easel. Hence it must be so.

In the fourteenth century, legend took on definitive form with the story of Veronica (the name was evidently a variant of Berenike) who, as Christ was on the way to Calvary, his face streaming blood from the crown of thorns, handed him a napkin which he pressed to his face and returned it bearing his image. The very napkin was alleged to have been found, and a vast number of illustrations show her either displaying the napkin or receiving it at the hands of the Savior.

The amount of actual depiction in the early centuries was very scant. During the first three hundred years, the period before

Constantine, we have few sculptures. Christ appears now as the Good Shepherd with long hair; and again bearded with cropped hair. The manner of depiction was taken over from pagan statues of Hermes or Endymion. As the Christians won adherents in the wealthier strata, sculptors were employed to carve reliefs for tombs. In these the Good Shepherd was a popular figure who, in that age of persecution, would protect his flock from the wolves.

In addition we have frescoes on the walls of the catacombs (tunnels for burial, miles in length) around Rome and other cities such as Carthage. Prior to Constantine, we have a depiction of Mary and the babe beside the prophet Balaam, who is pointing to a star in accord with his prophecy (Numbers 24:17), "A star shall come forth out of Jacob." There is a touch of realism in that the child is frightened by the prophet and is clinging to the mother. Mary's veil of virginity is faintly discernible.

Figure 3. The Good Shepherd (beardless, long hair)

Figure 4. The Good Shepherd (bearded, cropped hair)

Figure 5. Earliest Virgin and Child

Figure 6. Virgin and Child (4th century)

Figure 7. The standardized portrayal of Christ

In the fourth century, we have another fresco of the mother and child. Mary is on the way to becoming the Queen of Heaven. She has a necklace. Her veil is prominent. The hands are extended in the gesture customary in prayer. A figure in this pose was called an *orans.* The child on her knee appears to be older than the mother, not because the artist was unable to portray a child, but because the Son, the eternal Word, was God's agent in the creation of the world and consequently very much older than his mother.

At both ends of the mural we have monograms of Christ turned to face each other. The monogram consists of the first two letters of the name *Christ* in Greek: *Chi* which has the shape of our *X,* and *Rho* their *R,* our *P* in shape. The letters were joined in this fashion or in this . The use of the monogram can be dated on a coin of Constantine minted in A.D. 315. The coin shows Constantine crowned by a helmet containing the monogram.

A catacomb portrait of the adult Christ can be dated as late as the middle of the fourth century because of the haloes which cannot be traced before the year 340. The halo, also called a nimbus, was borrowed from pagan art where it was an aureole of light around the head of deity. Since the emperors were deified their portraits enjoyed its use. When Christian emperors abdicated as gods, they were still allowed circles around their heads, for "there is a divinity which doth hedge a king." The halo did not, however, imply full divinity and was given not only to Christ, but also to the saints. One observes on each side of the head the letters *Alpha* and *Omega,* the first and last letters of the Greek alphabet, because Christ *was* the beginning and the end. This depiction displays the form hereafter standard of Christ with beard and long hair—then the Syrian coiffure. Here we have the first of many examples of the adaptations of Christianity to local cultures. The new religion, Hebrew in origin, was in turn Hellenized, Romanized, Germanized, Celticized, besides being made conformable to the customs, costumes, and languages of Asia and Africa. To take root in a new environment, Christianity had to accommodate itself to modes and mores. Sometimes the pagan was made Christian; sometimes the Christian turned pagan. Amalgamation may spell enrichment or perversion. The adaptation in Celtic lands is a case of artistic enrichment without prejudice to content. The art of the Celts was abstract and decorative, making use of intricate interweavings of ribbons, appearing and reappearing in due alignment. When this technique was used to depict the crucifixion, the body of Christ looked like twisted coils of ropes. The advantage was that the Celt could say, "He is of us."

But what surprises us when we return to the earlier period is that the Christians, desirous of knowing how Christ appeared, should have left so little by way of depiction during the first three centuries. Much of course may have been lost. Marble sarcophagi coffins were too costly to be frequent. But the deepest reason may well have been official disapproval. The leaders of the Church did not countenance pictorial representation. Throughout Christian history there have been recurrent waves of aversion to art for religious purposes. We need to review the debates to understand the type of art which came to prevail.

In the early period, it was feared that a depiction of Christ would be regarded by pagans as an idol. Consequently, direct depiction was very much discouraged, and most of the Church fathers deprecated any sort of religious art. By the third century, the most liberal among them, Clement of Alexandria, would allow only symbols on signet rings for stamping. There might be a ship, the ark of salvation; or an anchor, shaped like a cross and a fish, because the letters of the Greek word for fish, *ichthys*, are the first letters of the Greek words meaning "Jesus Christ Son of God Savior."

Symbolism thus became a device for satisfying the craving felt for graphics without making idols. The New Testament offered several symbols: Christ was the Vine, the Good Shepherd, the Light

Figure 8. Celtic crucifix

Figure 9. *Ichthys* (fish) and cross

Figure 10. Christian seal

Figure 11. Phoenix symbol

of the World, the Lamb of God, the Alpha and Omega. John the Baptist saw the Spirit descending as a dove. Paul compares the Christian life to a race; the reward for the winner was a laurel wreath, which became a sign of the resurrection.

The Old Testament was a rich source of symbolism because of the belief that the persons and events of Israel's religious history prefigured Christ. His resurrection, the most popular theme in the catacombs, was intimated by Noah emerging from the ark, Jonah from the whale, and Daniel from the den of lions. Isaac carrying the wood for his own sacrifice typified Christ carrying his cross. Moses striking water from the rock was Christ giving the water of life. David beheading Goliath and Samson carrying off the gates of the city signified Christ defeating sin, death, and the devil.

Some symbols were taken directly from Graeco-Roman sources. A coin of Titus represented a dolphin wound around an anchor. A Christian took the anchor to be the sign of the cross and the dolphin, the sacred fish, betokening Christ. On a Christian seal, this device is shown with the word *ichthys* in mirror script, because the letters would be reversed in stamping.

Another example is the phoenix, in pagan mythology a bird which being burned rose again from the ashes as Christ from the tomb. On a Christian sarcophagus, we find the phoenix against a background of vines, with doves in the center pecking at the grapes, as if the Holy Spirit were hungry. In the center is a circle with the Alpha and Omega and the Christ monogram.

The two sepulchral monuments reproduced here present composites of symbols. In Figure 12, the central figure is an orans. The Good Shepherd appears in different poses at both ends. To our right of the orans on the top level, we have Adam and Eve and Noah; on the bottom level, the miracle of the loaves. To our left of the orans at the top, a figure with a scroll and then Daniel and the lions; at the bottom, the Jonah cycle with a dove on the gourd. In

Figure 13, at the bottom to our left, we see two men with a water
pot, then the Jonah cycle. Note above the sail the common pagan
representation of the wind. The whale appears twice, receiving and
emitting Jonah. Just above the whale to the right is Noah. On our
far right, we find snails, a crab, a lizard, two fish, a bird of some sort,
a boy running, and a man fishing (oblivious of the miracle). On the
top level on the far left, two women and three men are viewing a
figure swathed like a mummy. It may be Lazarus. The women would
be Mary and Martha, and the man with hand extended would be
Christ. In that case we do have direct depiction. This might well be
since this sarcophagus must be dated as late as the middle of the
fourth century, seeing that near the top of the sail is an angel with a
trumpet and wings, and wings on angels do not appear at an earlier
date. This angel is at the top of a rock from which Moses is striking
water of which men near him are drinking. Continuing to the right,
we have Jonah under the gourd and then a little shepherd with
two sheep.

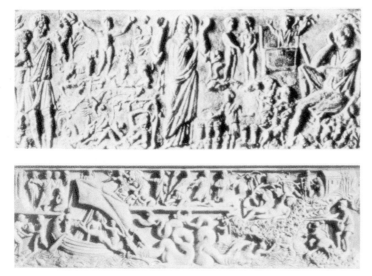

Figures 12–13. Symbols on Christian
sarcophagi

The symbols obviated the need for direct depiction, but even indirect suggestion troubled some because of the commandment not to make an image of anything "in the heaven above, the earth beneath, and the water under the earth." Taken literally, this spelled the death of art. The injunction as we have it in Exodus 20:4, according to the anthropologists, was motivated by fear of the sinister power of an image which was actually inhabited by the god. Israel's God was a jealous God and feared lest images of other gods would harm his people. And even an image of Yahweh himself was not a thing to be played with. When David was transferring the ark of the covenant to Jerusalem, and the oxen stumbled, Uzzah put forth his hand to steady the ark whereupon the Lord smote him dead. David was very angry with the Lord but took good care next time to assign the transfer to consecrated Levites who were able to carry the seat of holiness upon their shoulders with impunity.

Within the Old Testament itself there came to be a shift from the view that an image of the divine and holy *should* not be made to the view that it *could* not be made. We have another version of the commandment in Deuteronomy 4:12. There the reason given for the prohibition is that when God spoke out of the fire "you heard the sound of words, but saw no form: there was only a voice." In other words, God *cannot* be portrayed. How can the invisible be rendered visible? The Hebrews were right, said Hegel, for the proper medium for religion is poetry, not art; psalms, not statues or paintings.

But as a matter of fact, the Hebrews did not adhere strictly to this injunction and could justify themselves on the basis that Moses did not obey his own command, for did he not cast a brazen serpent and set it up in the wilderness that the sight of it might cure those bitten by serpents? The Christians excused Moses on the ground that the serpent signified Christ, but even more because God told Moses to make the serpent, and God is not bound by his own rules.

The Hebrews did have a religious art. There were images of the cherubim above the ark. The Jewish cemeteries of the Hellenistic age are replete with imagery borrowed and recast from pagan art, and the synagogue at Dura Europos has murals of the Old Testament stories.

Islamic art was more consistent in following the injunction of Moses. Islamic art is characterized by intricate patterns. The style is called arabesque. Yet the Muslims of Persia obviated the prohibition by drawing lines through the necks of men and animals to show that they had been decapitated. Certainly nothing in the heaven above, the earth beneath, or the water under the earth affords a model for active creatures with heads attached by epoxy.

Like the Jews, the Christians pointed to the exceptions to the Mosaic rule in the Old Testament. They also renumbered the commandments so that the prohibition of images became only an appendage to the command to have no other gods. If Yahweh were recognized as the only God, an image would be unobjectionable.

A difference in the numbering of the commandments has had a long history. From the beginning of the Christian era, all were agreed that the total must be ten. Philo, a Jewish scholar in Alexandria contemporary with St. Paul, made number one, "Thou shalt have no other gods," and number two, "Thou shalt not make any graven image." But St. Augustine put the two commandments together. Grouping two together at the start meant making two out of one at the end to keep the total of ten. But then all the intervening numbers were out of line. The fourth commandment on one basis was "Honor your father and your mother," and on the other, "Remember the Sabbath day to keep it holy." The Catholic and Lutheran churches have followed St. Augustine; the Orthodox churches and the Calvinists have preserved the numbering of Philo. So the Eastern churches have gone through two centuries of iconoclasm, while the Calvinists have allowed a cross but not a crucifix.

Figure 14. Cartoon against the Iconoclasts crucifying Christ afresh by giving vinegar to his image

The question of the numbering presented an obstacle to the union of the Protestant churches in southern India, because the Lutherans and Presbyterians were at odds as to whether the fourth commandment referred to parents or the Sabbath.

Of course the big question was whether the prohibition of images could be attenuated merely by making it merely an appendage. The Eastern churches were racked by the problem during the eighth and ninth centuries. Theological differences played a part. Christ had been declared by the Council of Chalcedon in 450 to be in two natures: human and divine. Two sects argued over this definition. The Monophysites (the name is from two Greek words meaning "one nature") claimed that Christ had only a divine nature. To portray him would then be to portray God, and this the East would never do. The Nestorians derived their name from the theologian Nestorius, who was excommunicated by the Council of Chalcedon on the charge that he so separated the two natures as to make Christ a split personality. If then only the human nature of Christ were portrayed, Nestorianism would be implied.

Political considerations were added to the theological. The image of the emperor in the East, as far back as the time of Sargon the Assyrian, had been regarded as containing the actual presence of the ruler. The image was able to issue edicts as if the emperor were there in person. This concept was taken over by the Roman emperors.

With a change of succession came a change of pictures in the villages. In the presence of such pictures oaths could be sworn. An 'insult to the image of the emperor was treason and rebellion. In Antioch during the time of Chrysostom, when the mob pelted the imperial statue, the emperor's vengeance on the city was forestalled only through the intercession of the saint. The Christian emperors, no longer claiming divinity, permitted images of Christ alongside of their own. But when the people preferred to swear before the Christ image, the emperor then asserted that the kingdom of Christ was not of this world and the images of Christ should be removed. The opposition was not to art as such. Hunting scenes were allowed and appeared even in churches.

The West was immune to the convulsions of the East but here, too, there were waves of iconoclasm. In the twelfth century, St. Bernard enunciated principles inimical to art in any form. He did grant that some concessions might be made to the common run by bishops. In a letter to Abbot William of St. Thierry, he states:

> Unable to excite the devotion of carnal folk by spiritual things, they do so by bodily adornments. But we [monks] who have now come forth from the people, we who have left all the precious and beautiful things of the world for Christ's sake, and have counted them but dung that we may win Christ, all things fair to see or soothing to hear, sweet to smell, delightful to taste, or pleasant to touch—in a word all bodily delights—whose devotion, pray, do we monks intend to excite by these things? [He complains of the costliness of church adornments.] The Church is resplendent in her walls, beggarly in her poor; she clothes her stones in gold, and leaves her sons naked.

Bernard was right that art in the form of architecture is expensive. The magnificent church at Assisi in honor of Lady Poverty could not have been built by Lady Poverty. The strictures of Bernard do not perhaps quite exclude all art, but only that which is pleasing. He might have been satisfied with blood-reeking crucifixes.

The great mystic of the fifteenth century, Nicolas of Cusa, enunciated principles of more far-reaching import. He ejaculated:

> O Lord, how admirable is thy face which a youth will conceive as young, a man as adult, an old man as aged . . . . O face, exceeding comely, whose beauty all who look upon it are unable to admire. Of all faces the face of faces is veiled and seen through a glass darkly, and unveiled is not seen unless one enter above all faces into a certain secret and occult silence where there is

> nothing of knowledge or concept of a face. This darkness, this
> cloud, this shadow or ignorance into which he who seeks thy
> face enters when he transcends all knowledge and concept,
> below which the face cannot be found save veiled, this very
> darkness discloses that the face is there above all veils. If one
> knows oneself in darkness, one knows that one approaches the
> face of the sun because the brilliance of its light casts a darkness
> over the eye and to the degree that it knows a greater darkness
> so much the more it enters in darkness into the invisible light.

The only possible graphic depiction of Cusa's concept would be
of a full moon on an intensely murky night.

Some of the sects of the Middle Ages objected even to the cross
without the body. Would one revere the gallows, it was argued, on
which one's father was hanged? During the Reformation, Zwingli
was outraged by the superstitions of the crowds on pilgrimages to
shrines with relics and holy images; nor would he tolerate altars
venerated with candles and incense. But he did not object to art as
such and let the stained glass windows remain when the images
were removed. Luther also protested only against superstitions and
was very fond of illustrations in Bibles. Calvin allowed the cross but
not the crucifix.

These various movements left their impact on art. In the East,
God was not portrayed save as a hand reaching down from above.
Rounded sculpture was banned; low relief was allowed. The test
was whether thumb and finger could get a grip on the nose. If so,
out with it. On these points the West diverged.

In both East and West, there was the feeling that the holy should
not be brought too close to man, and for that reason the divine man
on the cross should be clothed. The motive was not prudery, for in
the Rabula gospel, while Christ is draped, the thieves are naked save
for loincloths. A near naked crucifix at Rome in the fourth century
aroused an uproar, and as late as the eighth century, there is one
clothed. But eventually the near naked type prevailed in both

regions. Perhaps a feeling for historical accuracy was the reason. Crucifixions were not executed on the clothed..

The argument in favor of the images was derived all along the line from the doctrine of the incarnation. If the Word became flesh, why shouldn't the Word be depicted in the flesh? Spirit and flesh are never disjoined in all God's creation. The view that the corporeal is not a fit vehicle for the divine leads to a rejection of music through the ear, pictures through the eye, and sacraments through the mouth. The view that the flesh is the garment rather than the tomb of the spirit allows for the musical, artistic, and sacramental, with room for variety of emphasis.

In the use of pictures, the West was didactic, the East sacramental. In Europe, the picture was the textbook of the unlearned; in Asia, the icon was as much filled with the divine as the bread and wine in the Eucharist. A power dwelt in the icon. It was able to work miracles. So great was its hold on the people, that when a priest painted over the eyes of an icon, the congregation is alleged to have gone blind. To a westerner this sounds incredible, but in the East, faith can remove eyesight.

A little incident in my own experience gave me a feeling for the power of the image. I served in France during World War I with a Quaker unit of the Red Cross. After the Armistice, we stayed on for reconstruction. When we had finished the repair of dwellings in a village of the Marne, I took a bronze crucifix which I had found in the ruins to the mayor and asked whether I might have it. "Oh no, not that one," said he, "it was carried in the *Corpus Christi* procession. But here is a little one of lead which hung over the demolished school. You may have this one." This crucifix has hung in my office ever since. In successive moves, one leaden arm pulled away from the wood. So strong was the symbolism, that I could not bring myself to take a hammer and drive in a nail. In the end I used a little screw.

That same crucifix gave me a feeling for the horror experienced by some in the face of such materializing of the passion. Two boys of the Waldensian church called on me. This church was founded in France by Peter Waldo in the eleventh century. The rejection of the crucifix became an article of belief. When Mussolini required that a crucifix hang in every school, the Waldensians made such a protest that he allowed the presence of a Bible instead. One of my Waldensian guests shuddered on seeing the crucifix on my wall. The other calmed him by whispering, "It's all right. He has it for historical interest."

And now a word about the periods in Christian art. They are not so marked in the East as in the West. In the East, the forms of the Pantocrator and the Mother of God with her divine Son became formalized. There are varying degrees of spiritual intensity but no drastic changes in the modes of depiction. After the fall of Constantinople to the Turks in 1453, Byzantine art came to an end except as carried on in the Slavic lands notably Bulgaria and Russia.

During the age of persecution prior to Constantine, the main theme everywhere was the resurrection, and the chief representation of Christ, that of the Good Shepherd protecting his sheep from wolves. After the invasions in the West, we have the Romanesque period, with massive churches like fortresses. The stupendous tympana over the portals frequently carried portrayals of the last judgment, perhaps to warn the continuing violent invaders that they would receive divine retribution.

The twelfth century brought great changes. Christ hitherto portrayed as alive on the cross was now shown as dead; but coincidentally, he was depicted actually rising out of the tomb and not simply as already risen. The Renaissance brought a greater naturalism and introduced new techniques. The artists were sometimes more preoccupied with their new modes of depiction than with the subject itself.

The Reformation was not anti-artistic. In fact, one of the greatest religious artists of all time was the Protestant Rembrandt. But in general, the art to which the Reformation made the greatest contribution was music. The line runs from Luther to Bach. On the Catholic side during the late sixteenth and early seventeenth centuries, we find an intensely vigorous, revitalized Catholicism, marked by extravagance of expression.

The late seventeenth and eighteenth centuries showed a diminution in the productivity of religious art. Notably was this true of the Enlightenment with its rationalistic tendencies. The nineteenth century saw revivals with Blake and the pre-Raphaelites. The twentieth is marked both by a brutal realism and a defiant jubilation. The greatest vitality has been in the younger churches. Unhampered by traditional stereotypes, they have accommodated the Christian story to their own styles.

Having blocked out the main periods, let us now turn to the criteria of religious art. What makes art religious? Can art be religious? One has said that religious art is that which drives one to one's knees. Very well said! But one may still ask for what reason one is driven to one's knees. The cause may be terror, fright, contrition, awe, reverence, exultation. To fall to the ground out of sheer fright before a terrifying deity is indeed religious, but what sort of religion? We cannot pass judgment on the quality of religious art without passing judgment on the quality of religion. There are low forms of religion which view God as capricious, jealous, exacting, to be placated even by human sacrifice. There are more sophisticated forms which still conceive of religion as the manipulation of God. Art itself, if it take the form of constructing a superb cathedral for the sake of preferential treatment in heaven, is a prostitution of religion.

Appraisals of religious art depend on appraisals of religion, and appraisals of religion depend on the exercise of intelligence. Jesus said, "Love the Lord your God with all your heart, and with all your soul, and with all your *mind*." Religion is not just a wallowing in emotion, though there can be no religion without emotion. Some say that anything in religion is good which appeals to people and fills a need. No doubt child sacrifice and suttee appealed to people and filled a need. But what kind of need? Illusions fulfill a need and may help in weathering a crisis, but better it is to be utterly realistic and surmount despondency and despair through faith.

Yet it is true that there are levels of apprehension. Paul recognized the distinction between milk for babes and meat for the strong. Bernard, who decried images for monks spiritually advanced, allowed them for the carnally minded. Overly sweet and comforting religious portrayals are helpful to those who are not sufficiently robust to face the uglier aspects of life. Perhaps temperament has something to do with it. Historical circumstances certainly do.

Take Holman Hunt's painting of Christ as the Light of the World. My daughter showed this picture to one of her little boys when he was three or four. She said, "Now this is Jesus knocking at the door of your heart. What will you say to him?" He answered, "By the hair on my chinny-chin-chin you can't come in." I doubt that he meant to be contemptuous. He had learned one response to a knock and came out with it. But when I related this story to an adult, he roared with laughter and said that was just the way he felt about the picture. Yet a woman in her seventies said she had derived from it great inspiration.

Another point to remember with respect to a picture is its setting. A religious picture is much better able to drive one to one's knees if it is in a church, a hospital, or a home, than in a museum where it is designated by a number in a catalog and hangs beside a child playing with a parrot or a cubist anatomy dancing on a tightrope (if indeed it is a rope at all). A further point is that a religious picture must be understood. Pictures are not of themselves the

Figure 15. Holman Hunt.
Christ as the Light of the World

textbooks of the unlearned unless accompanied by some verbal instruction. This was brought home to me when, in Japan, I saw a traveling exhibition of Bulgarian icons. The one of doubting Thomas putting his finger into the wound of Christ was labeled, "Saint Tom's treachery."

Religious art must be substantive; it has to deal with religion. This does not necessarily mean that it must deal with specifically religious themes, but it must induce a religious emotion. The question is raised whether abstract art can be religious. Once a young man insisted to me that every religious emotion can be conveyed through the abstract. This I would contest. The abstract can convey infinitude, the immanence of the divine. Color combinations may lift one over the waves and clouds into the unfathomable. The arabesque style can induce composure. A stained glass window in the mosque of Suleiman the Magnificent evoked for me a deeper religious response than many a stained glass window crammed with symbolic details. Better soft light of manifold hues to lift one above the clutter of the senses.

The abstract can convey elevation. El Greco's baptism and resurrection might have been as uplifting if he had used spirals of ascending flames rather than the elongated figures of Christ, John the Baptist, and the angels. But some aspects of religion, and the deepest, I think, cannot be portrayed save through the human countenance: the contrition of the prodigal, the remorse of Peter, the amazement of the disciples at Emmaus, the compassion of the father falling on the neck of the prodigal, the agony of Jesus in the garden, the cry of desolation on the cross. These are all inner experiences, which reveal themselves outwardly through the expression of the face and the posture of the body. This is why the German critic Wolfgang Schöne said that the greatest religious art of our time is a depiction of the faces of devout worshippers.

Christian art must be distinguished from religious art in general.

Figure 16. Wilhelm Leibl. Worshippers at prayer

29

Figure 17. From Tissot's depiction of the flight into Egypt

A Cézanne or a Manet suggests an identification of the spirit of man with God immanent in all reality. It is religious, but it is not specifically Christian. A Christian may respond to it indeed. So also may a Hindu, a Buddhist, a Muslim, or a Jew. This is universal religion. Mysticism, whether focused on nature or inner experience, is universal. Christianity is particular. It affirms that God in a unique way was manifest, incarnate in Jesus of Nazareth in the days of Herod the king. Christian art, in consequence, has to be largely historical, even though Christ transcends history.

The necessity of conforming to history imposes certain limitations. Since particular human beings are to be portrayed, the use of line is indispensable, mere color combinations will not do. In this sense abstract art is excluded. It can create a mood; it cannot depict an event.

The manner in which an event is portrayed can vary. Some artists have sought to be faithful to history by putting the entire life of Christ in a Palestinian setting. This was the method of the Catholic artist Tissot early in this century. However, the majority of artists have transferred Palestine to their own countries, using local colors, costumes and faces. Thus to universalize Christ is legitimate, but this method itself imposes restrictions. Jesus may be given a face that is brown, bronze, white, black, or yellow because there are men of these hues, but scarlet or emerald green will not do. I think Van Gogh, for example, has gone too far in his *Pietà*. Over against the deep blue of Mary's robe he has given Jesus red hair. This is too contrived, for in Jesus' day, there had been no crusaders in Palestine to leave a heritage of red hair. Or is the point that Van Gogh, whose own hair was red, was depicting himself as the "Man of Sorrows"?

A distinction between religious and secular art is that the religious does not make beauty a goal. There may indeed be a charming Madonna, an adorable Christ child; but in religion, the ugly is sometimes more appealing. I find myself aghast at the repulsive ugliness of some of the pietàs, but obviously they have appealed, because they call to mind the sufferings of Christ, who, being in the form of God, humbled himself, assuming the form of a slave with "no beauty that we should desire him."

In a religious painting, skill in craftsmanship must never call attention to itself. This is the area in which the artists of the Renaissance were severely tempted to flaunt their skills, whereas icon painters of the East worked only with stereotyped forms and fixed media. The western artists experimented with perspective, contrasts of light and shade, juxtaposition of colors, oil versus tempera. The artist, experimenting with a new technique, was sometimes carried so far away as to allow the technique to obtrude itself above the central intent. That same artist might, however, through a deepening religious experience arrive at a point of making his craftmanship unobtrusive. There are examples to come in the cases of Dürer and Caravaggio.

Thus, while the artist should not be obsessed with the display of his skill, he should not renounce it, as Picasso did in drawing the left hand of Christ upon the cross. The drawing befits the kindergarten. That an artist able to equal the ancient masters in the delineation of a hand should revert to childhood is a part of the renunciation of culture. The way to escape from sophistication lies not in renunciation of skills, but rather in the consecration of the highest skills to lofty ends. When I was a child, I drew as a child, but now that I have become a man, I do not scribble.

Nor can the Christian artist recover the quaint simplicity of a less sophisticated age. This applies to the use of symbols. All Christian art has to be symbolic in a sense. The Christian is not interested in portraying animals like the Assyrians, plants like the Egyptians, and human bodies like the Greeks. He is interested in conveying the sense of divine reality through symbols. In the

Middle Ages, symbols were quaint, persuasive, sometimes farfetched. One never knew whether an apple was just an apple or the apple Eve gave to Adam; whether water was plain water or the water of which if a man drink he shall never thirst. The Renaissance made symbolism esoteric and sophisticated.

In the nineteenth century, the Pre-Raphaelites invested naturalism with all too contrived allusions. Millais' boy Jesus in the carpenter shop shows him holding up his hand accidentally cut by a nail. Mary is kissing away the hurt. John the Baptist is bringing a bowl of water. The noses of a flock of sheep appear at a window waiting to be fed. Similarly, there is Holman Hunt's Jesus in the carpenter shop. As he stretches himself his shadow falls on the wall in the shape of a cross. In my feeling it were better to let the carpenter shop be just a carpenter shop which the viewer can invest with meaning.

My own preference is for drawings with great economy of line subtly suggesting realities beyond appearance.

The master here for me is Rembrandt.

Figure 18. Sir John Everett Millais. Jesus in the workshop

Figure 19. Holman Hunt.
Jesus the carpenter

Figure 20. Rembrandt van Rijn.
The boy Jesus in the Temple

33

1
NATIVITY

H LITTLE TOWN OF BETHLEHEM,
why did it happen in you?" Jesus was of Nazareth. The evangelist
Luke explains that "a decree went out from Caesar Augustus" that
all the empire should be taxed. And thus every man had to report
in his own village. This, for Joseph, meant Bethlehem, though he
worked in Nazareth. He, alone, need have returned, but he took
with him, "Mary his betrothed, who was with child." As they
approached Bethlehem, her time came. He tried to find room for
her in an inn, but "there was no room." So she delivered her firstborn
son in a stable, wrapped him in swaddling clothes, and laid him in
a manger.

In this succinct account there are four episodes: the census, the
journey to Bethlehem, no room in the inn, the birth in the stable.
The first three have received scant treatment in Christian art. I have

discovered no depiction of the Emperor Augustus decreeing the census prior to the fourteenth century. The explanation lies in changing circumstance. Luke had no hesitancy in assigning to the emperor an incidental role, since when the gospel was written, the Roman government was protecting the Christians from Jewish attacks. But when, in A.D. 62, the Emperor Nero initiated a series of persecutions, the Christians came to regard the emperor as the man of sin whom the Lord Jesus "would slay with the breath of his mouth." This attitude, of course, changed when the Emperor Constantine became a Christian, but there was still little point in giving to his pagan predecessor a role in the drama of redemption.

How different was the situation when Figure 21 was done in the West in 1339! At that time, the emperors, the kings, and the princes of the city-states were trying to throw off the overlordship of the popes in temporal affairs. Only a few decades before this date, the poet Dante had written a treatise on monarchy in which he claimed, quite erroneously to be sure, that the Holy Roman Emperor of his day was directly in the succession of that Emperor Augustus who instituted the census, and was commissioned by God to set the stage for the birth of the Savior. Emperors, therefore, receive their authority as immediately from God as do popes, and popes should not meddle in temporal affairs. At that juncture there was point in playing up the role of Caesar Augustus.

The journey from Nazareth to Bethlehem has received nothing like the attention given to the flight into Egypt. No artist, to my knowledge, has discovered here what was seen by Luther, for whom the journey was the supreme example of Mary's humility. She, who might have been conveyed in a golden chariot with a gorgeous equipage, trudged her weight over the hills in winter on foot. "The artists," said Luther, "give her a donkey. The gospels do not." Figure 21 gives her not only a donkey, but also an ox. Did the artist want to make sure of having both animals at the crib? Legend says

Figure 21. Decree of Augustus and journey to Bethlehem

Figure 22. Jan Metsys.
Rejection at the inn

Figure 23. No room in a Chinese inn

that Joseph hoped to sell the ox in Bethlehem in order to pay the tax for which the census was instituted. An incidental detail is that Joseph wears the headgear of European Jews in the fourteenth century.

The theme of no room in the inn apparently received no treatment until the sixteenth century. The early Christians, for whom there was no room in the Roman empire, suggested their experiences through Old Testament analogies. After Constantine, there was room for Christians in the inn. The first depiction of rejection is from the brush of a painter in the Netherlands, Jan Metsys, banished from Antwerp for fourteen years on suspicion of heresy. No room for him in the inn. The next examples are from our own time. There is one from China where the Boxer rebellion and the Com-

Figure 24. Ralph Coleman.
A gentle refusal

munist pressure closed the inn at times. Figure 24 comes from the era of sweetness and light in the United States. The host seems to be saying, "My dears, I'm dreadfully sorry, but I just haven't any room." Then comes one from the period of upheavals. The host can be interpreted as the Establishment saying, "Get the hell out of here." Was the artist alienated from a "Christian" culture which sends Mary to the stable to bear the Prince of Peace?

The birth in the stable as a separate item received little treatment until after the transfer of the commemoration from the sixth of January to the twenty-fifth of December. The reason for the sixth of January will be explained in the chapter on the Wise Men. The transfer can be dated by a ruling of Leo I, the bishop of Rome, in 354. The change was made in order to provide a counter-attraction to a pagan festival on that date. December twenty-fifth, on the old calendar, was the winter solstice, when the sun commenced "his"

Figure 25. James Reid. A brutal refusal

upward course. The sun was a god: Apollo in the West; Mithras in the East. He was the god of the Persians, and there was a real chance that he might become the god of the Romans. Oriental religions, often imported by slaves, were then inundating the Roman West. Shrines of Mithras, commonly grottos, have been found not only in Rome but also along the great frontier rivers—the Euphrates, the Danube, and the Rhine. The blitz unearthed a mithraeum under London.

Shortly before Constantine, the Emperor Aurelian attempted to make Mithraism the religion of the empire. Though he failed and Constantine gave his favor to Christianity, Mithraism did not die out at once. Constantine did not suppress paganism, and when, a few years after his death, Christmas was set on the birthday of Mithras, the rivalry of the religions was still acute. The danger was not fanciful that recent converts on the day of the celebration

39

Figure 26. Ox and ass without Mary and Joseph

Figure 27. Mary recumbent with ox and ass tussling

would rejoin their pagan friends and then never return to the church. (The principle of counter-celebrations is still operative in our own day. A rabbi explained to me that in order to keep Jewish children within the fold at Christmas, the comparatively minor Jewish festival of Hanukkah, commemorating the reconsecration of the temple by the Maccabees, has been played up.) Christians, then, in the middle of the fourth century, were called upon to worship not the sun but "the Sun of Righteousness with healing in his wings."

The pictorial representations of the birth from this time forward vary as to the place. The birth takes place in the West in a shed; in the East, in a grotto as in the shrines of Mithras. Whatever the style, the baby Jesus had to be there, but sometimes Mary and Joseph are omitted and only the ox and the ass appear. The reason is that in the early period, the ox was taken to represent the Jews, the ass, the Gentiles, but lately coming to Christ. In the Middle Ages, the relationship was, however, reversed. The ox stood for the Christians, the ass for the Jews, and the tussle between the animals for possession of the swaddling clothes of Jesus was not simply slapstick but the conflict of the Church and the synagogue.

Ordinarily, of course, Mary and Joseph are there. The normal representation down to the fourteenth century was that of Mary prone in bed after the pangs of childbirth. Joseph in a corner, his chin on his hand and his hand on his staff, brooded for a thousand years.

Emphases shifted with the cult of the Virgin in the twelfth century. The new elements were in line with the burgeoning of legend at all points. The yarns of the apocryphal gospels were amplified and embellished and quite new fantasies introduced. In winter there was a rose a-blooming. At midnight on Christmas eve, all the animals in the woods knelt in reverence. The Angel Gabriel brought the Virgin a wedding contract to be signed with God the Father. It is not extant. Mary was elevated and emancipated from menial chores. Joseph was assigned domestic tasks. We find him

Figure 28. Joseph cooking

Figure 29. Maid and midwife

Figure 30. Joseph lights a fire

Figure 31. Joseph dries
the diapers

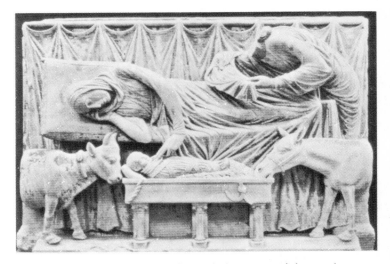

Figure 32. The tender touch

Figure 33. The sparkling babe

cooking, then drying the swaddling clothes. Mary did not take on outside employment but devoted herself the more to the babe. A stone relief at Chartres delicately portrays her tender touch.

The great leap forward in her portrayal came in the early fourteenth century, when legend was amplified by vision. St. Brigit of Sweden was given to see exactly what happened in the stable. Mary in ecstasy in a kneeling upright position delivers the child without pain and continues kneeling in adoration. The child radiates glory. Joseph is given a candle to hold, perhaps to show how feeble is its light in comparison with that of the babe. But by and by he is given a lantern instead.

Figure 33 depicts a scene in which all of the elements are combined. The sun and the star take part. The shepherds are on a distant hill. The Wise Men are approaching with a long equipage. Mary kneels before the sparkling babe. Joseph cups his right hand over a candle whether for warmth or to shield the flame. An angel on the roof of the shed displays a scroll with *Gloria in Excelsis,* and the ass brays a lusty *"Hosanna."* Here then we have the type prevalent in Renaissance painting.

The theme of the baby emitting light was handled with great delicacy by Correggio, by Rembrandt, and by Gerard van Honthorst. No longer does the child look like an incandescent candle on a birthday cake. Visitors form a ring around the manger. The faces of

Figure 34. Gerard van Honthorst. The Light of the World

Figure 35. Crèche

all are equally lit from in front, because the light emanates from the light of the world.

Depiction of the birth took on a new popularity with the introduction of the crèche. St. Francis is thought to have been the originator. With some of the brothers, he took an ox and an ass into the woods and there constructed a manger. Now in Christian lands models of all the participants are made in wood, ceramics, and stone—some crude, some exquisite. Even in New England, where Christmas was banned until shortly after the Civil War, one will now find a twinkling tree and beneath it the Holy Family on the village green.

Modern artists, inhibited sometimes by tradition, treat the theme frequently with independence and imagination. All of the participants and accoutrements of the scene are native to whatever the region. Within each area, there is a great variety of representation. Examples are given here from Africa, India and Korea.

Figure 36. David Chituku. African nativity

Figure 37. A. D. Thomas.
Indian nativity

Figure 38. Ki-Chang Kim.
Korean nativity

2
SHEPHERDS

HEPHERDS WATCHING their flocks by
night were terrified when the whole hillside was ablaze with light.
An angel reassured them with the good news that on this very day
in Bethlehem, the city of David, a savior had been born who is
"Christ the Lord." The sign was that they would find a babe wrapped
in swaddling clothes and lying in a manger. "And suddenly," says
the evangelist, "there was with the angel a multitude of the heavenly
host."

Luther commented, "A multitude—as many angels as there are
blades of grass on earth and all singing that Christ is Lord and Savior.

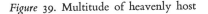
Figure 39. Multitude of heavenly host

You would have thought that some of them would have gone to the baby Jesus to take him a golden candle or a featherbed or some warm water. This is something we cannot understand till we find out at the resurrection." Such a reflection would scarcely come to a modern even if he were endowed with Luther's imagination. Luther, like the generation of the New Testament, casts visions, dreams, and special insights into the form of angelic visitations. But the development of artistic representation of angels was rather slow. They do not appear in the catacombs, and they did not acquire wings until the middle of the fourth century. The Bible gives wings to cherubim and seraphim, but not to angels. The wings were borrowed from the winged "victories" of the Hellenistic world. Sometimes they were given even to saints. An Ethiopian ascetic, having amputated a leg, was compensated with six wings. In the Gothic period, wings were so rampant that sculptors introduced specialization with one

Figure 40. Winged Ethiopian ascetic

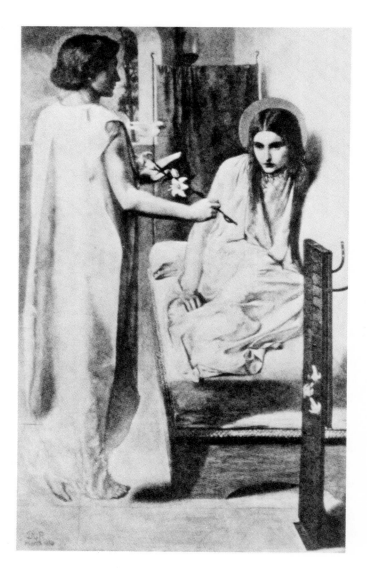

Figure 41. Dante Gabriel Rosetti. Wingless Gabriel

shop making bodies and another wings. By the time the parts were assembled, sometimes the wings did not fit.

After the Enlightenment, many came to feel that wings did not fit at all. Rossetti, in his painting of the annunciation, omits wings. In our day, those who are repelled by such concretizing of the supernatural may nevertheless respond to such depictions in a time when they did fit into an entire world view. And there are depictions from that period which suggest an interpretation more congenial to the taste of a scientific age. We have a portrayal of the encounter of angels and shepherds from around the year 1000 in which a huge angel extends a hand toward a shepherd who responds with a salute. One has the feeling that an electric spark will leap from hand to hand.

Figure 42. "Electric spark"

Figure 43. Shepherd as piping Pan

In the depictions of the shepherds, the artists sometimes reverted to the bucolic tradition of pagan antiquity and showed a shepherd looking like a piping Pan. More commonly however, each land gave the shepherds the faces of its own peasants—rough, coarse, worn with toil. These "hewers of wood and drawers of water" were shown in their simplicity as perceiving that which is hidden from the wise and prudent (Figure 44). In an illustration of the coming of the shepherds in Indonesia, the whole scene is naturally placed in a native setting. To a westerner, the ox and the ass look like deer.

Figure 44. Peasant shepherds

50

Figure 45. Wajan Turun.
Indonesian shepherds

Figure 46. Marcus Topno.
Indian shepherds

3
WISE MEN

FTER THE SHEPHERDS came the Wise Men from the East, having seen a star which betokened the birth of a king of the Jews. They came inquiring if they might worship him. The star had not indicated the place. This they learned by asking King Herod, whose own wise men said Bethlehem. The king at once sent them to search out the child, whom he meant to destroy as a rival to his throne. The Wise Men were now guided by the star to the manger. They fell down and worshipped the child, presenting gifts of gold, frankincense and myrrh. Warned in a dream not to go back to Herod, they returned to their own country by another way.

Figure 47. Babe in the manger and Child on the knee

This incident has enjoyed a wide vogue in Christian art, partly because it is picturesque, and partly because it meant recognition of Christ by the Gentile sages at a time when, in David's city, there was no room in the inn. The event was commemorated on the sixth of January. This is the feast of Epiphany, meaning "the manifestation of the glory." Any event in the life of Jesus could be so described. Four events were assigned to the day: the birth, until the celebration was transferred to the twenty-fifth of December; the baptism, assumed to have taken place on Jesus' thirtieth birthday because the gospel of Luke says that he was then about thirty; the coming of the Wise Men; and the miracle of turning water into wine at the wedding at Cana. The inclusion of this wonder was what determined the choice of January sixth as the date, for on that day water stored in the temples of the wine god Dionysus turned into wine. Christians did not hesitate to take over pagan usages to invest them with deeper meanings. On the same date as Dionysus, Christ transformed water into wine. At the same time, the neophyte was transformed in the spirit through the water of baptism.

When the transfer of Christmas to December twenty-fifth occurred, an interval of twelve days was set between the birth and the coming of the Magi. Could they have made the journey from Persia, their assumed land, in so short a time? Some suggested that they arrived two years later on the same date, because Herod commanded the slaughter of all the children of Bethlehem up to the age of two. Because of such conjectures, the artists sometimes showed Jesus at different ages on the two occasions. Figure 47 shows Jesus as a babe in the crib on the left, but seated on his mother's lap as a child on the right. In Figure 48, he is old enough to reach for the gift.

Figure 48. The Child grasps the gifts

Figure 49. Varied numbers of Wise Men

+SCS BALTHASSAR +SCS MELCHIOR +SCS GASPAR

Figure 50. Ravenna mosaic

The very idea that Christ could grow was more congenial to the East than to the West. Of course, neither could deny that he "grew in wisdom and in stature." But the West, which stressed the divinity of Christ, found it hard to believe that God could be two or three weeks old. The East stressed the humanity of Christ and the deification of man. There is an incarnation of God to a degree in all of us, they held. We are like a tree in bud. Christ is a tree in full leaf and flower. He became man in order that we might become God. We are "participants of the divine nature" (II Peter 1:4). "When we see him we shall be like him" (I John 3:2). He had to hallow every stage of life to show us that whatever the age we may be fashioned into his likeness.

The artists naturally followed the scriptural account where it was clear and specific. At many points it was not. The number of the Wise Men is not given. They were assumed to have been three because they brought three gifts, but each of a dozen might have brought three gifts. In the portrayals we have first two, then four. Only later did the number three become standard.

Figure 51. The Three Kings

Figure 52. Geoffrey Tory. Black Caspar

The names of the Magi are not given in the gospel. We find them around the beginning of the sixth century in the Hellenistic East. The earliest extant written source is a mosaic at Ravenna, though the names may have been added later than the date of the mosaic (ca. 550). As for the derivations, Melchior is clearly from the Hebrew *Melek Or*, meaning "king of light." Balthazar is the name of the king of Babylon, mentioned in the book of Daniel. Caspar or Gaspar is thought to be a corruption of the Indian Gundaphorus, the king under whom the Apostle Thomas is believed to have carried Christianity to India.

The Wise Men were not called kings until around 450, and the designation did not become common until the beginning of the seventh century when the liturgy of Gregory I conjoined the account of Matthew with the verse in the 72nd Psalm: "May the kings of Tarshish and of the isles render tribute, may the kings of Sheba and Seba bring gifts."

When did Caspar become black? This happened first in a nativity play in France, but not then as a mark of honor. Caspar was the buffoon, his blackened face set off by brilliant clothes, his lean body loaded with heavy gold chains, his tousled hair capped by a gaudy hood. By the fifteenth century, he emerged as a colleague with the others. This was because when Africa was discovered to be a continent, Europe, Asia, and Africa were apportioned among the Magi. The depiction of one as black met at first with some resistance in Italy, where Giorgione repainted a dusky Caspar making him white. But in the sixteenth century in France, Geoffrey Tory showed two Wise Men fully draped, but gave Caspar only a headband, shorts, and garter to make him unmistakably black (Figure 52).

The above embellishments are additions—rather than contradictions—to the Scriptures, but there is one point at which the artists definitely disregarded the account of the gospel that the Wise Men "fell down" before the Christ child. In the pictures, they stand

Figure 53. The angel pushes the star

or kneel only for the presentation. The reason is that in the pagan art of antiquity, those who prostrated themselves were suppliants before the king rather than the bearers of gifts.

All of these details are trivial compared with the great significance of the event. The adoration of the Magi meant the homage of one religion to another. The three came from Persia, the land of Mithras. One of them brought incense, which suggests that he may have been a priest of Mithras, though no early Christian writer makes the claim. In any case, the adoration of the sages from the land of Mithras cannot have been without significance as indicating a recognition of Christianity.

Even more important was the character of the star, because it spelled the end of magic. From the East, the home of astrology, the cult of the sidereal had cast a pall of fatalism over the West. Man's destiny was believed to have been settled by conjunctions of the planets or configurations of the heavenly bodies. But the star that guided the Wise Men was no ordinary star; it did what God directed. Close to the earth it moved, waiting while the Wise Men rested, and then guiding them to the spot where the young child lay. This star must have had intelligence. It must in fact have been an angel. On occasion, it is depicted as an angel or even as the baby Jesus. Sometimes an angel pushes the star like an auxiliary astronaut.

Figure 54. Jesus as the star

Such a star was a servant of God, whose sway was now manifest over all the stars, no longer to be regarded as demonic forces to be averted by magical incantations. And so magic was doomed. Christianity had overcome the sinister occult forces not by scientific discovery of their non-existence, but by the religious insight that Christ was "victor o'er the dark domain." The very stars were subject to his will, and man was delivered from their thrall.

The adaptations to diverse cultures are apparent in the changes of costume and the modes of travel of the Wise Men. At the outset we have the Persian mantle. Incidentally, when in 610 the Persians captured Bethlehem, they spared of the Christian mosaics only the one of the Magi because of the Persian mantles. In the mosaic at Ravenna (Figure 50) we have a striking blending of cultures. The names of oriental origin have an inscription in Latin, though it may have been added later. Again we meet the Persian mantles and now, no longer the Roman knee skirts, but Persian trousers like those of captives taken in the Persian wars. Though the mosaic was executed under the rule of Theodoric the Ostrogoth, the style is Byzantine. When the eastern emperor Justinian recovered Ravenna, his regime was glorified by new mosaics in one of which the hem of the robe of the empress Theodora was decorated with the scene of the Magi.

As for the modes of travel used by the Wise Men, each country placed them in its own setting. From Persia they came on camels. In the West they had horses; and after the eighth century, stirrups, lately introduced from the Mongols. One picture shows them returning to their own country in a boat.

A still more amazing example of the mingling of cultures is found in "Frank's" casket, an ivory box with carved sides and lid. It has been assigned to Northumbria around 700, but a recent study points out that the language of the runic lettering is that of the Anglian form of Anglo-Saxon. This insight dates the casket at the middle of the sixth century, when there was, as we know, a colony

Figure 55. Theodora's robe

Figure 56. Return by boat

Figure 57. "Frank's" casket

of refugee Angles in Merovingian Gaul. King Theudebert sent one of them as an ambassador to the court of Justinian, where he may have learned the art of ivory carving. The scenes on the different sides are Romulus and Remus, Titus' capture of Jerusalem, an adventure of Achilles, and the story of Balder, the Nordic vegetation god.

On the left of the panel in Figure 57 we have the Nordic myth of Wayland the smith, who was forced to work solely for the king by having his tendons cut at the knees. He revenged himself by luring the king's sons to pluck birds and bring him the feathers, from which he made wings for his escape. Then he killed the boys and made goblets out of their skulls. He induced the king's daughter to bring him a beaker of beer, which he drugged and gave her to drink. Then he assaulted her and fled. In the panel he stands over his forge holding tongs, a decapitated prince at his feet. The daughter appears twice, once bringing the beaker and once reaching for the drink. To the right are the plucked birds.

On the right side of the panel, we have the Wise Men in pantaloons; the one in front is carrying a vessel topped with three coins, indicating the gold; the next carries a pot of burning incense; and the third is bringing the myrrh. The word *MEXI* inscribed above is a form of *Magi*. Mary and Jesus are enthroned faces forward, eyes turned to the right—thus combining the Syrian frontal and the Hellenistic profile styles. The star is a large rosette. The Wise Men are oddly preceded by a goose, perhaps to match the birds in the other half.

Who did this? Was the artist a pagan who at Constantinople had picked up one more bit of mythology, or a Christian who thought that all history led up to Christ, and who wished perhaps to contrast the cruelty of the smith and the generosity of the Wise Men? Such are the conglomerations arising from the confrontations of cultures.

Figure 58. Gentile da Fabriano. Italian Magi

In the process, the pagan element may be Christianized and the Christian may be paganized. What is the criterion for saying which is which? The Middle Ages faced the question. The legend relates that St. Martin was once confronted by Satan in the guise of Christ resplendent. The saint scrutinized him and then asked, "Where are the nail prints?" The apparition vanished. Where are the nail prints? But this test cannot be applied mechanically. Christ had no nail prints during his ministry. The test must be the mind of Christ, the blazing indignation against the den of thieves, compassion for the downtrodden, forgiveness for the penitent, and lowliness over against the lordly.

During the Renaissance, depictions of the Wise Men reached a pinnacle of elaboration. We have scenes as ostentatious as a White House reception. In Figure 58, the Italian nobility throng the

canvas and chat with each other oblivious of the child. After the sixteenth century, there was a decline in artistic portrayals of the scene. This may have resulted from the dropping of the mystery plays by Catholics and the discontinuance of the Feast of the Three Kings by Protestants.

In the twentieth century the younger churches have found the theme congenial, with, of course, their own modifications. Figure 59 is an example from Iran, the ancient Persia. The Magi are portrayed as members of the priestly class. As in the earliest representations, they have the Persian mantles and arrive on camels.

Figure 59. Agha Behzad. Modern Persian depiction

A delightful example of the adaptation of the story of the Wise Men to local circumstance is found in a drawing by a North American Indian in the period following the Revolutionary War. The Magi arrive in canoes. The first carries a copper artifact, the symbol of wealth; the second, a vessel with materials for a ritual dance; the third, a staff, the sign of authority by which the bearer was entitled to sit with the council.

Figure 60. American Indian treatment

Figure 61. Japanese version

Figure 62. Adoration of the Zulu Wise Men

4
SLAUGHTER
OF THE
INNOCENTS

EROD, WHEN HE SAW that he had
been mocked by the Wise Men, resolved not to be foiled and
ordered the killing of all the children in Bethlehem up to the age of
two years. The episode received considerable attention in Christian
art, because the innocents were regarded as the first Christian
martyrs and were assigned the twenty-eighth of December in the
calendar of saints.

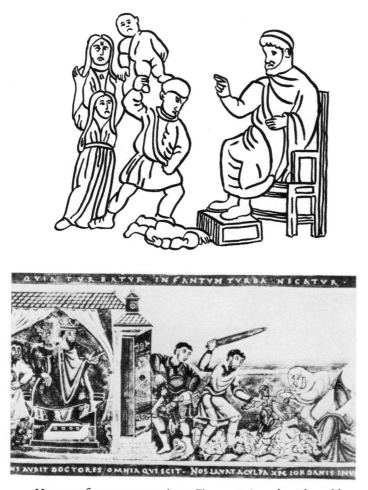

Figure 63. Slaughter of the Innocents. Fifth-century depiction

Figure 64. Tenth-century depiction

Here are four representations. Figure 63 is early. The soldiers are in Roman costume, but kill after the manner indicated in Psalm 137:9: "Happy shall he be who takes your little ones and dashes them against the rock." The Gospel Book of the German Emperor Heinrich III in the tenth century (Figure 64) includes Herod also.

Figure 65. Thirteenth-century depiction

Figure 65 comes from France in the thirteenth century. Soldiers in coats of mail kill by the sword. The one here has grabbed the hand of the child in his mailed fist. The sword is plunged. The face of the child has an expression of trust.

Poussin, in the seventeenth century, gave a very dramatic rendering. Since then, an age inured to violence has not thought this one worthy of especial note.

After the sixteenth century, depiction of this scene is passed over. The Victorian age of sweetness and light shielded itself from gore. One would have thought that the twentieth century, which has butchered so many innocents, would have revived the theme. (A movie has—the one on the gospel of Matthew. The soldiers with spears are perched on a hill about to swoop.) Television has shown us many pictures of the writhing napalmed children of Vietnam without ever a reference to Bethlehem.

Figure 66. Nicolas Poussin.
Seventeenth–century depiction

5
FLIGHT INTO EGYPT

LIGHT INTO EGYPT was Joseph's recourse when apprised in a dream of Herod's intent. The episode was popular in art because of the legend that the Holy Family destroyed the idols in Egypt. Since nothing save the flight is recorded in the gospel, legend has filled the gap. Joseph is alleged to have eluded the pursuit of Herod's soldiers by the ruse of asking farmers sowing grain to tell inquirers that the family sought had passed at the time of sowing. Then, during the night, the seed came to full maturity by a miracle. In another tale, when Joseph could not

Figure 67. Martin Schongauer.
The bent palm

reach the dates on a palm, angels pushed down the branches within
reach.

   The artists thoughtfully assumed that the family on so long a
journey would have been in need of a rest and diverted themselves
by depicting the interlude in the midst of the delightful landscapes

71

Figure 68. Lucas Cranach the Elder.
Rest on the flight

Figure 69. Mary teaches Jesus to walk

of their own countries. In the sixteenth century, Cranach has the family resting by the base of a tree about which a ring of cherubs dance gleefully. Two rascally cherubs up in a branch are robbing a bird's nest, as if fledglings were not also innocents.

The family stayed in Egypt until the death of Herod. How old that made Jesus we cannot say, because the precise date of his birth cannot be determined. So Christ may indeed have been born Before Christ. The artists assumed that he became old enough for Mary to teach him to walk with a stroller and for Joseph to give him a "piggyback."

Figure 70. Joseph gives Jesus a "piggyback" ride

6
BOYHOOD
AT
NAZARETH

ON THE DEATH OF HEROD, the family returned to Nazareth. From then on, only one episode is mentioned of Jesus until his baptism at the age of thirty. The one incident is of the twelve-year-old lad in the temple disputing with the doctors. His parents had taken him to Jerusalem for the Passover, then started back without him, supposing he was travelling with another family.

Figure 71. Boy Jesus in the Temple

After a day, not finding him, they went back and at length discovered him in the temple discussing with the rabbis. His mother
scolded him roundly. "What on earth do you mean by letting us
worry ourselves nearly to death for three whole days?" He answered
that he must be about God's business. Mary accepted the answer
and he went back with them "and was subject to them." His
parents gave him his liberty and he accepted their rule.

Figure 72. Jesus helps in the shop

Figure 73. Jesus helps with the washing

Figure 74. Detail from Diego Rivera's "Vaccination"

But this is not the point which has attracted the artists. They have centered on the precocity of the lad. The encounter with Mary has been glossed. Sometimes she is shown flurried at the door. Perhaps the closest to a genuine depiction is a little fifteenth century woodcut. Mary is scowling. Jesus extends his hands persuasively.

As for the life in Nazareth, legend frequently shows Jesus helping Joseph in the carpenter's shop. Less frequent are the scenes of help to Mary. Jesus brings her a tub of water for the washing and holds the spindle for her weaving.

By way of local adaptation, a fifteenth century German shows Mary teaching Jesus to walk with a stroller, while a modern American depicts him being vaccinated. Must he have done everything we do?

From this infelicity one turns to the words of Erasmus in his meditation on Jesus composed for a boys' school:

> Perhaps boys may better think of Jesus as a boy, lying in swaddling clothes in a manger, while angels sang, shepherds adored, the animals knew him, the star stood over where he lay, Herod trembled, Simeon embraced, Hanna prophesied. O humble simplicity! O sublime humility! How can thoughts conceive or words suffice to express his greatness? Better to adore than to seek to explain. What then shall we do, if John the Baptist said he was unworthy to unloose the latchet of his shoes? Strive, my dear boys, to sit at the feet of Jesus the teacher.

77

7
BAPTISM

OR THE BAPTISM, FOUR ELEMENTS
are requisite: Jesus, John the Baptist, the dove, and water (the amount
is disputed). The first depiction, from the catacombs, has these
elements. The dove is the key to the interpretation. Otherwise, one
might think that this was merely one man pulling another up an
incline.

More details were added in time, and the treatment became
stereotyped. Figure 76 shows an example with the hand of God
above, releasing a dove bearing a jug of oil to be poured on the head.
John the Baptist lays on his hands. We have thus, three cardinal
liturgical acts: baptism with water, anointing with oil, and laying-on
of hands. John has a halo, but not Jesus. Could this be a harking back
to the view that Jesus became the Son of God only at his baptism?

Figure 75. Catacomb depiction of the
baptism

Figure 76. Traditional depiction of the baptism

Figure 77. Jordan personified

Some depictions show a little old man in the river. He is the river god, for the Hebrews personified Jordan as the pagans did Neptune. The Psalmist says "What ails you, O sea, that you flee? O Jordan that you turn back?" (Psalm 114:5). The river god was evil. Christ with one hand is warding him off, while with the other blessing the water. Here is the recognition that water is both the friend and the enemy of man. There is the water of a pool in the burning sand, the water in which Naaman bathed and was cured, the brook after which the hart pants, the river which makes glad the city of God. And there is also the water of the flood which destroyed all but the household of Noah, the water of the sea which would have engulfed Jonah save for the whale and Peter save for Jesus. Baptism, then, is the symbol of the water blessed by Christ to deliver man from the tempest of evil. The significance of baptism is best expressed in the language of the Apostle Paul, who said that in baptism we die to sin and rise to newness of life. The baptism and the resurrection are thus associated.

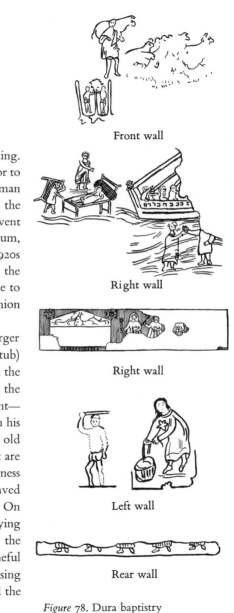

Front wall

Right wall

Right wall

Left wall

Rear wall

Figure 78. Dura baptistry

Baptism is the theme of the oldest extant Christian building. It is the baptistry of the church at Dura Europos, which dates prior to 236, the year the city was taken by the Parthians. Dura was a Roman outpost on the Euphrates. When the Parthians laid siege, the inhabitants threw up earthworks on the inside of the walls to prevent sapping. The embankment buried a synagogue, a mithraeum, and a Christian church. Excavations were conducted in the 1920s under the auspices of Yale University. By agreement with the Syrian government, the synagogue was removed stone for stone to Damascus; the mithraeum and the baptistry came in similar fashion to the Yale museum.

The baptistry was a room in a private house adjoining a larger assembly hall. This is plainly a baptistry because there is a font (tub) in front. But there is no depiction of any baptism. The fresco on the wall above the font affords the reason. Here we have contrasted the old Adam—that is, Adam and Eve with the tree and the serpent—and the new Adam—namely, Christ as the Good Shepherd with his flock. This is in line with Paul's counsel that we must put off the old Adam and put on the new. On the right wall as we face the font are scenes displaying the power of Christ to deliver man from sickness and death. The paralytic takes up his bed and walks; Peter is saved from the waves; women come to the tomb on Easter morning. On the wall opposite, we have David as the type of Christ slaying Goliath, and we have the woman at the well. One observes the contrast, perhaps not consciously intended, between the baneful water, which threatens to engulf Peter, and the water of blessing in the case of the Samaritan woman, to whom Christ promised the water of which if a man drink he will nevermore thirst.

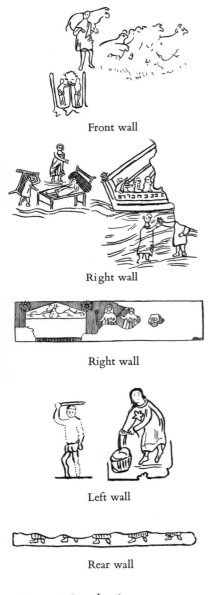

Front wall

Right wall

Right wall

Left wall

Rear wall

Figure 78. Dura baptistry

Some details of the Dura baptistry are worthy of note. The sheep (here, actually rams) are not grouped around the Good Shepherd like students around Aristotle. Some are grazing. As the grass is cropped, they are moving on beyond the frame of the picture. Christianity has broken the bounds of Greek art which, to rationalize life, encloses a fragment. Christianity deals with a reality that breaks through a frame—the flock is moving toward pastures unexplored.

There are touches of local realism. The rams have the long tails still common in the Orient. The ship from which Peter has stepped out is one of the trading vessels used in the Persian gulf. The hairdos of the women approaching the tomb are in the style of the court of Zenobia of Palmyra. An odd point is that the women approaching the tomb are given space for five, whereas in our gospels there are never more than three in one account. This artist was following a compilation of the four gospels called the *Diatesseron*, meaning "made out of four." A fragment of this work by the Syrian Tatian was found in the ruins. Along with symbolism we have, then, touches of local usage.

A partial destruction of the frescoes enables us to do a little allegorizing of our own. The body of Christ saving Peter is gone. The hand remains. Even so, we, who cannot see his face, feel his saving grip. On the rear wall there are rows of feet without bodies. What a symbol of the multitudes of Christians throughout the ages whose features have passed into oblivion but without whose moving feet the gospel would never have come to us!

A well known depiction of the baptism from the seventeenth century is that of El Greco. He has included the traditional features. At the top we have not simply the hand of God but God Himself.

82

Figure 79A. El Greco. Baptism

Figure 79B. El Greco. Resurrection

We find Jesus, John, the Jordan and, of course, the dove. Several angels are holding the clothes. There is no novelty here. It is to be found, rather, in the elongated figures characteristic of El Greco. The spiral forms and clustered angels give a sense of vibrant elevation, of aspiration, of rising from the Jordan to the throne of God. But why the baptism? One derives the same impact from El Greco's resurrection, and for that matter, even from his painting of Toledo in storm. It might be entitled "A city that is set on a hill cannot be hid." The specific subject does not matter for El Greco. In the baptism, in the resurrection, and in nature itself, he discovers the yearning of the soul to rise from its dead self to higher things. And that, too, is the essential message of the Dura baptistry. Each is designed to assist the way of ascents.

8
MIRACLES

IRACLES RECORDED OF JESUS in the gospels are numerous. Three only are depicted here. The multiplication of five loaves and two fishes so that five thousand were fed illustrates his generosity. The curing of a leper shows his compassion. The casting out of a legion of demons from one possessed demonstrates his power. This last miracle, called that of the Gadarene swine, has been highly controversial. The gospel relates that in the region of Gadara, Jesus encountered a demoniac too strong to be bound. When Jesus commanded the unclean spirits to

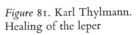

Figure 80. Loaves and fishes

Figure 81. Karl Thylmann.
Healing of the leper

Figure 82. The Gadarene swine

leave him, the man begged that they might be sent into the swine. Jesus complied, and two thousand pigs plunged into a lake and were drowned. Criticism started at the time. The owners of the animals were less pleased over the cure of the man than displeased over the loss of such a herd. Jesus was asked to leave. Curiously, the age of rationalism fastened its critique on this miracle, the easiest of all to explain on rationalistic grounds, assuming that the demoniac went into such a frenzy that the pigs stampeded over a cliff. Voltaire scoffed that Jesus sent the demons into swine in a land where swine were not raised.

In the nineteenth century, Thomas Huxley took up the critique, not on scientific but on moral grounds. The wanton destruction of another's property, said he, is a grave misdemeanor, of which either Jesus was guilty, or he did not perform the miracle at all. Huxley preferred the second alternative. Gladstone defended the historicity and said that the loss served the owners right since by raising swine they were transgressing the Mosaic commandment against pork. Huxley countered that the Gadarenes were not disobeying Moses because they were Gentiles.

Figure 83. Sadao Watanabe.
Japanese treatment

9
PARABLES

REACHING BY PRECEPT and parable
was characteristic of Jesus, though one may be certain he did
not preach from a fifteenth century German pulpit. Two of his
parables are noticed here. The first is that of the Prodigal Son.
The story is that the younger of two sons asked to have his part
of the inheritance in advance. The father let him have it, and he
went to a distant land where he squandered all in high living.
When his funds were gone, no one would befriend him, and he
found nothing to do but become a swineherd and eat garbage with

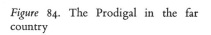

Figure 84. The Prodigal in the far country

Figure 85. Albrecht Dürer. Contrition

Figure 86. Peter Opitz. Repentance

the pigs. He came to his senses and reflected that his father's hired hands had it better. He would go home, admit that he had done wrong to his father and to God, and ask to be allowed to be a hired man. He started home. When he was still a long way off, his father saw him and ran to him. Erasmus commented that he who had the greater love was the first to spy the other. The boy began his little speech, but the father cut him off, threw his arms about him, kissed him, and called for a robe and a ring and a fatted calf for a banquet. The comment again of Erasmus: "Now remember, this father is God."

There are three episodes here. The first is the high living in the far country. The second is the repentance of the Prodigal Son portrayed by Dürer and by a contemporary artist in East Germany. The contrition in these faces exhibits admirably what abstract art cannot convey. The inner experiences of the human spirit call for the face and the posture.

Figure 87. Lukas Ch'en. Return

The most significant depiction of the return of the Prodigal comes from China. Under the old regime a father sitting on his veranda would never have budged a toe to show a sign of recognition to a returning wayward son. But this father is running across the courtyard to embrace him. The gospel here has supplanted the cultural tradition of millennia.

Figure 88. Van Gogh. The Good
Samaritan

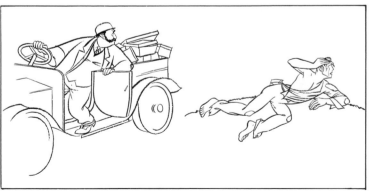

Figure 89. Thomas Derrick.
Modern treatment

The point of the parable of the Good Samaritan is that "the Jews had no dealings with the Samaritans," and pilgrims to the Passover, if they had to pass through Samaria to reach Jerusalem, could not be assured of friendly treatment. In the parable, a Jew is traveling from Jerusalem to Jericho when he is set upon by thieves who attack, rob him, strip him, beat him, and leave him half dead. A Jewish priest and a Jewish Levite going that way pass him by, but a Samaritan stops, treats his wounds, puts him on his beast, takes him to an inn, pays the expected bill, and promises on his return to take care of any extra.

For this parable only two examples of portrayal have been selected. The first is by Van Gogh. It is vastly superior to his *Pietà*, where he made the hair of Christ red to contrast with the blue robe of Mary. His Good Samaritan does not depend at all on color, but solely on line drawing. The man left half dead by the robbers is too weak to lift a leg to help himself onto the back of the beast. The Samaritan is straining as if he were lifting a 150-pound sack of cement. His back is twisted and his left leg braced. To fit this picture, the word of the gospel should be changed to read not that he "set" him on his beast, but "heaved" him on.

The second example comes from our own century. The Good Samaritan drives up in his old Ford, sees the poor fellow sprawled across the sidewalk, and gets out to help. The Good Samaritan in this example is manifestly a Jew.

10
TRIUMPHAL ENTRY

ALM SUNDAY IS THE NAME given to
the day when Jesus rode in triumph into Jerusalem. The gospels
record how throngs hailed him, strewing branches and their clothes
in his path. They shouted "Hosanna! Blessed is he who comes in
the name of the Lord. Blessed is the kingdom of our father David
that is coming!" John's gospel is more explicit. The crowd had
assembled because they had heard of the raising of Lazarus, and they
cheered not simply the coming of the kingdom of David, but Jesus
himself as king. One can understand why the charge of political
insurrection could be made plausible to the authorities.

The delineations of the event vary slightly as to details. In the
West, Jesus is astride the ass after the Roman manner. His feet often
nearly touch the ground. In the East, he rides sideways and looks
much like the Christ in majesty of the icons. Matthew's gospel
mentions a colt as well as the ass (Figure 92). Often, diminutive
figures, both young and old, are up in a tree to watch the procession.
Enthusiasm for strewing garments has induced one fellow in
Figure 91 to pull all of his clothes over his head.

Figure 90. Triumphal Entry.
Western style

Figure 91. Triumphal Entry.
Eastern style

Figure 92. The ass and the colt

In the later Middle Ages in the West, Palm Sunday processions were much in vogue. Either a man rode a donkey or a wooden carving of a man on an ass was mounted on wheels and trundled through the streets. In Germany, this figure was called the *Palmesel*, meaning "palm-ass." The practice was popular especially in Germany and Switzerland. The Reformation swept all of this away as superstition and idolatry. The *Palmesel* was "drowned" in the lake of Zurich and others were burned, but a number have survived. There is a fine example at the Metropolitan Museum in New York. The only survival today of the festivities is the distribution of palm leaves.

Figure 93. The *Palmesel*

11
ANOINTING AT BETHANY

LOOKING ABOUT THE TEMPLE with
an eye to cleansing it on the morrow, Jesus then went to Bethany to
spend the night in the home of Mary, Martha, and Lazarus. John's
gospel tells us that Mary took a pound of costly ointment and,
having anointed the feet of Jesus, wiped them with her hair. Judas
complained of the extravagance, saying that the ointment might
have been sold and the price given to the poor.

The other gospels relate the story with some variants. The
anointing is recorded as having taken place in Bethany, but the
woman is not named. Complaint of the expenditure was made not

Figure 94. Anointing with oil and tears

by Judas alone, but by all of the disciples. These episodes have been conflated with still others. A woman, who was a sinner, washed the feet of Jesus with her tears and wiped them with her hair. She is not named but has been equated with Mary Magdalene, of whom we are told only that seven demons had been cast out from her. She was present before the cross, and to her the risen Lord appeared in the garden. She in turn has been identified with Mary, the sister of Martha and Lazarus. From a historical point of view, accuracy is necessary, but a religious message can be carried by a character in fiction. The point here is that Jesus was deeply comforted, as death

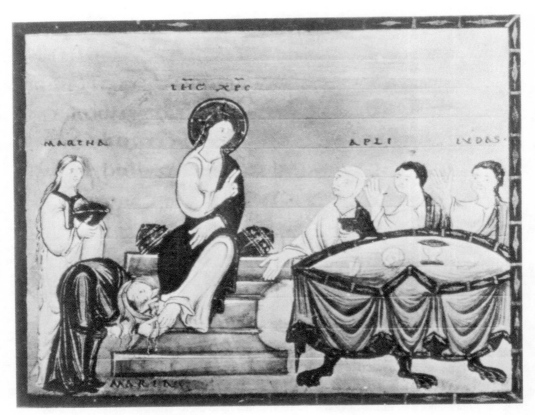

Figure 95. Chiding the apostles (*Apli*)
and Judas

Figure 96. Strasbourg's depiction

approached, by an act of uncalculating devotion. There are times when charity, which can never reach all, may be extended lavishly to one in an hour of crisis.

We find here in our first example (Figure 94), a combination of one woman at the top pouring ointment on the Master's head and another at the bottom drying his feet with her hair. Our second example shows Jesus, even while Mary is drying his feet turning from her to chide the unctuous charity of the apostles and Judas. A sixteenth-century depiction from Strasbourg has the city's sign of the stork on the chimney.

12
CLEANSING OF THE TEMPLE

LEANSING THE TEMPLE WAS ONE
of Jesus' great acts of defiance. It could have precipitated the crucifixion if the Romans had heard not only that Jesus had been hailed
as king, but that he had also assaulted the regime of the temple
hierarchy operating under Roman auspices. The merchants expelled
were those who battened on the needs of pilgrims for kosher coins
to buy the animals for sacrifice.

The time of the cleansing is assigned to different occasions in the
gospels. John places it at the beginning of the ministry, but had it

Figure 97. Christ driving out the money changers

happened then one may doubt whether there would have been a ministry. Mark differs from Matthew and Luke by a day. The evangelists were concerned for significance rather than sequence.

The scene, despite its historical importance, has received but slight graphic representation. The Christians appear not to have been eager to play up defiance of authority. A mosaic in the Byzantine style from the twelfth century shows no particular feature to indicate why the theme appealed to the artist. The same may be said of Giotto's treatment in the fourteenth century. They may have depicted the episode simply because it was in the gospel.

During the Renaissance, the Humanists preferred to use Hercules as the figure who cleansed the Augean stables rather than Christ who cleansed the temple. Holbein even portrayed Luther as Hercules. But the Protestant reformers made use of the scene in their polemic against the papacy. Melanchthon issued a pamphlet entitled *The Passional of Christ and Antichrist,* a series of satirical cartoons showing, on one side, Christ driving out the hucksters, and on the other, Antichrist, the pope, raking in the gulden from the indulgences.

Figure 98. Pope raking in the gulden

Figure 99. Rembrandt van Rijn.
Retreat of the money changers

For human delineation, no depiction equals the power of Rembrandt's portrayal: the outraged indignation of Christ, the terror and, at the same time, the avarice of the money changers grabbing the coins before flight.

In the modern period, the episode has been adduced to prove that Christ would approve of taking part in war. Did he not display a fiery wrath? Did he not use a whip? Indeed yes, but a whip of cords is not an arquebus, a bayonet, or a bomb. But I have seen no modern portrayals of Christ driving out the Kaiser, Hitler, Stalin, or Mao. Has secularism gone so far that an appeal to the example of Christ is not convincing? Or is the point that history is "bunk" and we need no warrant from the past? Or is there such a heightened sense of history as to make us realize that no present situation has an exact parallel?

13
WASHING THE DISCIPLES' FEET

URING THE EVENING prior to his betrayal, Jesus washed the disciples' feet and instituted the rite of partaking of wine and bread in remembrance of him. The foot washing is mentioned only in John's gospel, which has no account of the institution of the Eucharist, though it uses its language in connection with the miracle of the loaves. John relates that as the disciples were assembled, Jesus girded himself with a towel and washed their feet. Peter protested at first, but when Jesus told him that otherwise

Figure 100A. Peter's protest

Figure 100B. Peter tested

Figure 100C. Gesture of shoe removal

he could have no part in him, Peter wanted to be washed, head and all.

In the interpretation of the footwashing, the East differed from the West in emphasis. The East stressed the forgiveness of sins and regarded the washing as a rite of purification, like baptism. For the disciples, in fact, the footwashing appears to have been the only baptism. That is why Peter wanted to have his whole body washed. See him pointing to his head in Figure 100A.

Preparation for baptism was necessary in the case of converts and so also, according to the pictures, for the footwashing. In Figure 100B, Christ is shown probing Peter's leg to test his worthiness. Another feature of purification was the removal of shoes. This depiction became so stylized that the gesture sufficed even though the apostle had no shoes to remove (Figure 100C).

Figure 100D. Christ's humility

In the West, the emphasis was on the humility of Christ and the duty to follow in his steps. In Figure 100D, Christ is shown kneeling as a sign of condescension, though an angel serves as a deacon. The great stress was laid on the words of the Master, "If I then, your Lord and Master, have washed your feet, you also ought to wash one another's feet, for I have given you an example." So great was the emphasis on the call to imitation, that sometimes in the depictions, the actual washing is not taking place, and Christ is delivering an exhortation (Figure 100E).

Figure 100E. Christ's example

Figure 101. Sadao Watanabe. Japanese
treatment

Figure 102. St. Louis IX of France washing the feet of beggars

There is a striking treatment of the theme by a modern Japanese artist, Sadao Watanabe. He has done many of the gospel themes in a style reminiscent of the manuscript drawings of the Carolingian period. There is a quaint wistfulness in the faces. He is fond of repetitive designs like those of the old Celtic art. One notes here the lines of the hair, the fingers, and the waves.

The theme of footwashing became institutionalized. The monks washed each other's feet. Kings, emperors, and popes annually washed the feet of beggars. Luther swept all this away as a piece of ostentatious humility. Zinzendorf, the founder of the Moravian church, revived the practice among the German Pietists. The Church of the Brethren today in addition to the Lord's Supper observes also the rite of footwashing. Though this practice is an anachronism in an urban culture, the washing of feet by a group can be a symbolic moving experience.

14
LAST SUPPER

AST SUPPER, OR LORD'S SUPPER, is the term applied to the meal that Jesus shared with his disciples before his arrest. Because he spoke then of the bread as his body and the wine as his blood, the occasion has been regarded as the practice called by Catholics, the *Mass*, by Protestants, usually the *Lord's Supper,* and by all, the *Eucharist*. The word *Eucharist* means, in Greek, "a thanksgiving," because Jesus "took bread, and when he had given thanks, he broke it." Of all the sacraments, none is more frequently observed than this. Christmas, Epiphany, and Easter come but once a year. The Mass is available to Catholics every day, and communion is available to Protestants sometimes every Sunday, sometimes monthly.

The significance of the Lord's Supper is set forth in the New Testament with three emphases. Paul, writing to the Corinthians, stressed the past. He protested against their making it too jovial an occasion and reminded them that it was a remembrance of the night on which the Lord was betrayed. There was, at the same time, a future reference, for the commemoration was to be continued

Figure 103. Agapé with baskets of loaves

until his return (1 Corinthians 2). In another passage, Paul emphasized communion with Christ. "The cup of blessing which we bless, is it not a participation in the blood of Christ?" (1 Corinthians 10:16). Luke's gospel has Jesus say that he will no more drink of the fruit of the vine till the kingdom comes (Luke 22:18).

The liturgy of the Anglican church includes all of these elements. "Take and eat this in remembrance that Christ died for thee." Here is commemoration. "And feed on him in thy heart." This is communion. "The body of our Lord Jesus Christ . . . preserve thy body and soul unto everlasting life." The reference is future.

Pictorial representation of the Lord's Supper as such is to be found only after the time of Constantine. The reason is that the Eucharist—the consecration of the elements—was not separated from the common meal, the *agapé,* or love feast for some time. This is why Paul had to admonish the Corinthians not to eat and drink to excess. We do have a number of representations of the love feast in the catacombs, but these are not to be interpreted as portrayals of the historic Last Supper. They depict the actual love feasts of the Christian congregations. The number of the participants varies, perhaps six, perhaps seven. The presiding figure is not Christ, but the leader of the congregation. On the table, along with bread and wine, we frequently find fish, because the symbolism of the Eucharist in John's gospel occurs in connection with the miracle of the loaves and fishes. In some of the catacomb frescoes we see baskets of loaves alongside, like the baskets of the bread left over from the miracle.

The wine was sometimes mixed with water. This practice explains the inscriptions in Figure 104. Directions are given to two women: Irene, meaning "peace," and Agapé, meaning love. Since the name *Agapé* is foreign to our usage, we might call her Charity. The inscriptions then read: "Irene bring hot," that is hot water. "Charity mix," that is, mix the water with the wine.

Figure 104. Agapé with mixture of water and wine

Figure 105. Ethiopian Lord's Supper

Figure 106. Richard West. American
Indian Lord's Supper

Figure 107. School of Giotto. Christ as priest

When the Eucharist did become a separate act with no meal, the form of the representation followed the manner of the liturgical practice. In the West, the common mode of seating was at a rectangular table after the manner of a Roman banquet. In the East, we sometimes have a circular form. So it is in an example from Ethiopia. Curiously, we have the very same arrangement by an American Indian, who portrays the disciples as if squatting about a camp fire. During the early Renaissance, the Lord's Supper was so far accommodated to liturgical practice, that the School of Giotto showed Christ as the priest, giving the paten and cup to the apostles. Note

Figure 108. Judas and the blackbird

that Judas has a black halo. Often he was shown with the devil as a little blackbird entering his mouth. A similar picture of Christ administering the rite as priest comes a century later from the Netherlands.

The great revolution in the manner of depiction came in the late fifteenth century at the hands of Leonardo da Vinci, who turned from the liturgical to the historical style. He was not portraying the love feast or the Mass, but the behavior of the disciples as he conceived it to have been at the time. They are not communicants waiting to receive the paten and the cup, but are rather dramatically interlocked, their positions determined in part by considerations of composition. The centrality of Christ is highlighted not by elevation, but by placement in the frame of a window. The groups on either side are oriented toward him but with criss-crossing diagonals. A figure on our right is so contorted, that while his face looks to the left, his arms are twisted to the right and his body is at a diagonal to his neighbor.

This delineation has met with various responses. Goethe was enthusiastic over it, for he saw not the institution of the Eucharist, but the consternation of the disciples when Christ predicted that one of them would betray him. Berenson, the great art critic of our century, was so repelled that he could scarcely bring himself to appreciate the composition. "But," he added, "I am a northerner." This may be the clue. An Italian cannot even telephone without gesticulation. This difference may account for the way in which the original scene was imagined. The gospel says that the word of Jesus caused searching of heart. The disciples were actually so unsure of themselves as to ask, "Is it I?" A northern reaction would have been stunned silence. Our judgments are, of necessity, subjective, but we must not reject that which speaks to another.

There are some treatments which, on all counts, are utter travesties. This stricture applies to the work of Tintoretto in the late

Figure 109. Dieric Bouts. Similar Netherlandish treatment

Figure 110. Leonardo da Vinci. The animated Lord's Supper

Figure 111. Il Tintoretto.
The Supper in a tavern

sixteenth century. He treated the theme several times and always introduced details from the scullery. The example shown here places the scene in the dining hall of an inn. Attention directs itself not so much to the blazing head of Christ, as to the woman in the foreground who appears to be washing eggs or vegetables and to the cat trying to get a lick. Why didn't Tintoretto paint tavern scenes outright like Franz Hals or Jan Steen?

The conflict between delight in craftsmanship and concern for religious meaning is very evident in two depictions of the Last Supper executed by Albrecht Dürer. Figure 112 was done while he was experimenting with the techniques of perspective developed in the Italian Renaissance. Observe the skill with which he has rendered the receding lines in the cupola above the head of Christ. Note the minute delineation of the ringlets in the hair of the apostles and of the folds in the cloth hanging from the table. Theologically, Dürer here anticipates the exuberance of the Baroque. Christ is haloed in ecstasy by a broad aureole and is abstracted from the group.

Figure 113 was done after Dürer's own religious life had been deepened by Luther. The craftsmanship is no whit inferior but is not obtrusive. The halo is much smaller and Jesus is engaged in conversation with the disciples. On the table stands the chalice which the Protestants gave to the laity.

Figure 112. Albrecht Dürer.
Lord's Supper (1510)

Figure 113. Albrecht Dürer.
Lord's Supper (1523)

Figure 114. Lucas Cranach the Younger (1515–86). Luther and companions at the Lord's Supper

During the Reformation the Protestants were guilty of what is regarded by a secular age as monstrous irreverence. They put themselves in the seat of the apostles, except Judas. This treatment was not altogether new. Gentile da Fabriano had given the faces of the Medici to the Wise Men. But to seat Luther and Melanchthon in the seats of a Peter or a John is going rather far. One must remember, however, that these men lived in a perpetual Passion Play. Dürer felt no irreverence in painting himself as the Man of Sorrows, surrounded by the instruments of the Passion. An account of Luther's trial at Worms was a parody of the gospel of John's account of the trial of Jesus. Pilate was Charles V, Caiaphas, the archbishop of Mainz, and Christ was Luther himself. The artist Hans Cranach (Figure 116) gave his features to Simon of Cyrene carrying the cross and Lucas Cranach portrayed John Frederick, Luther's prince, standing to hear a sermon with a wooden cross resting on his shoulder. These men were living Luther's lines, "Let goods and kindred go. This mortal life also." Every day they were playing roles in a perpetual Oberammergau.

A treatment by a German artist at the close of World War II appeals to me. The faces of the apostles are those of German peasants. The seat of Judas is vacant. No more the startled incredulity of the prediction of the betrayal. It is on the way to fulfillment. Now is the hour of the searching of hearts.

Figure 115. Albrecht Dürer
Dürer as the Man of Sorrows

Figure 116. Hans Cranach. Cranach as Simon of Cyrene carrying the cross

Figure 117. Lucas Cranach. John Frederick carries a cross

Figure 118. Michael Ell. Modern German version

15
GETHSEMANE

ETHSEMANE IS THE NAME of the
garden on the Mount of Olives to which Jesus withdrew with his
disciples after the supper. According to Luke's gospel, he left the
disciples to watch while he went aside to pray. His prayer was,
"Father, if you are willing, remove this cup from me; nevertheless
not my will, but yours be done." In agony, he prayed more earnestly,
and his sweat was like drops of blood. Coming back to the disciples,
he found them asleep.

John's gospel sounds as if he were correcting Luke's version.
For according to John, Jesus says, "Now is my soul troubled. And
what shall I say? 'Father, save me from this hour?' No, for this

Figure 119. Christ in Gethsemane

purpose I have come to this hour." Whereas Luke says that the Master sweats blood, John assures us that he did not even ask to be spared. Surely the Lukan account must be correct. Had Jesus been so composed, the agony would never have been invented. Jesus was a martyr who might have escaped, not simply a victim. He might have withdrawn earlier to the regions of Tyre and Sidon. Instead, he set his face steadfastly to go to Jerusalem, though the outcome was clearly foreseen. Nevertheless, in the moment of confrontation he cried out to be spared. John thinks in the light of eternity. Jesus the Word, through whom all things were made, was fulfilling the destiny from which he would not shrink. So it seemed after the event had assumed cosmic proportions. But we are not to forget that Jesus was a man "tempted in all things even as we are."

All accounts make plain that the struggle was the more agonizing because Jesus faced it alone. The disciples were asleep. Luke tells us that an angel comforted him. This is the mode of concretion common to the era. One would be inclined to believe that Christ in his humanity saw no heavenly visitant. He was comforted simply by the sense of God's nearness and undergirding power. One cannot, however, complain of the artists who show the angel. This was the mode of the New Testament.

There is a simplicity and quaintness about early depictions. Here are two examples: one from the West, one from Ethiopia. In both, a little angel holds a cup and a cross. Jesus looks up rather placidly

Figure 120. Ethiopian depiction of the agony in the garden

121

Figure 121. El Greco's treatment

Figure 122. Doré's engraving

122

while the disciples sleep. The same theme treated by El Greco wears an air of unreality. The angel appears with a cup as elegant as the goblet of Benevenuto Cellini. There is surprise, rather than agony, on the face of the Savior. And do we need an angel at all? The inner struggles of the soul are best conveyed by an expression of the face or a posture of the body. Doré's engraving has both expression and posture and at the same time heightens the isolation of the Master by placing the sleeping disciples in the shaded foreground. An American woodcutter achieves an impressive effect by posture. I find myself even more moved by the work of an American Indian, who has conveyed the inner struggle primarily by the facial expression.

Figure 123. James Reid. Woodcut

Figure 124. Richard West.
Christ as an American Indian

16
ARREST

ESUS BETRAYED BY JUDAS was
arrested in the Garden of Gethsemane. There are several stages: the
betrayal, the severing of the ear of Malchus by Peter, the servant
of the high priest, the naked flight of the young man, the remorse
and suicide of Judas.

The gospel accounts vary somewhat. Combining them, we
learn that Jesus was met by armed soldiers sent by the priests. Judas
identified Jesus with a kiss and Jesus asked, "Do you betray with a
kiss?" The ear of the servant of the high priest was cut clean by
Peter, whom Jesus rebuked and then restored the ear. John's gospel
indicates that Judas betrayed, not Jesus' identity, but his location.
When the soldiers arrived, Jesus asked them for whom they were
looking. "Jesus of Nazareth" they answered. When he replied
"I am he," they fell to the ground. Recovering, they arrested him.

Figure 125. Giotto di Bondone.
The Judas kiss

Figure 126. Gustav van de Woestijhe.
Modern version of the Judas kiss

Figure 127. Peter severs the ear of
Malchus

Figure 128. Judas hangs himself

A young man whose clothes were seized fled naked. And Judas, when Jesus was condemned to crucifixion, in remorse hanged himself.

Several points call for comment. The conclusion has been drawn that Jesus could not have approved of participation in warfare because he told Peter to put up his sword with the word, "He who takes the sword shall perish by the sword." But one should not deduce an absolute from this saying, any more than one should find a warrant for crusades in the cleansing of the temple. The ethic of coercion in the thought of Jesus requires a study of all his sayings, his deeds, and the tenor of the New Testament.

The motives of Judas have been variously assessed. According to the New Testament, he was actuated by greed. He was politically naïve and did not grasp what the result of the betrayal would be. When he found out, he threw back the money and took his life. This is too simple for some modern interpreters. One suggestion is that Judas did regard Jesus as the Messiah, who would summon legions of angels to drive out the Romans. The cleansing of the temple appeared to be the occasion. But when Jesus did nothing but sit and teach in the temple, Judas thought to force his hand. Surely, having been arrested, he would bring in the angels. When Jesus did not, Judas hanged himself.

A more recent interpretation is that Judas, once devoted to Jesus, had come to agree with Caiaphas that the excitement of the crowds about Jesus would prompt Roman intervention and spell the end of Jewish home rule. It is "expedient," said Caiaphas, "that one man should die for the people." Judas felt that he was the one who must betray his friend for the sake of national security. But having done so, he could not live with himself. These are ingenious interpretations. The simple gospel account holds together without them. But in any case, the kiss of Judas has become the symbol of the most galling treachery.

17
PETER'S DENIAL

ETER WAS THE ONLY DISCIPLE to suffer the ignominy of having denied his Lord. The reason was that of all, he was the bravest. While they fled, he followed to the courtyard of the high priest before whom Jesus was to be tried. On the way to the garden, Jesus had predicted that all would fall away. Peter proclaimed that he would die rather than deny. Jesus told him that before the cock crowed, he would three times deny him. During the examination, Peter tried to elude notice by joining a

group warming themselves before a fire in the courtyard. A servant girl and bystanders, observing his Galilean accent, insisted that he was a disciple. He added to denials on oath that he never knew the man. The cock crowed, and Peter went out and wept bitterly.

This incident shows the revolution effected by Christianity in the classical world. Erich Auerbach has given poignant expression to this new understanding of the tragic and the sublime:

Figures 129–130. Peter and the cock

> Peter, whose personal account may be assumed to have been the basis of the story, was a fisherman from Galilee, of the humblest background and humblest education. The other participants in the night scene in the court of the high priest's palace are servant girls and soldiers. From the humdrum existence of his daily life, Peter is called to the most tremendous role. Here, like everything else to do with Jesus' arrest, his appearance on the stage—viewed in the world-historical continuity of the Roman Empire—is nothing but a provincial, an insignificant local occurrence, noted by none but those directly involved. . . . Yet how tremendous it is, viewed in relation to the life a fisherman from the Sea of Galilee normally lives, and what . . . goes on in him! He has left his home and work; he has followed his master to Jerusalem; he has been the first to recognize him as Messiah; when the catastrophe came, he was more courageous than the others; not only was he among those who tried to resist but even when the miracle, which he had doubtless expected, failed to occur, he once again attempted to follow Jesus as he had followed him before. It is but an attempt, halfhearted and timid, motivated perhaps by a confused hope that the miracle by which the Messiah would crush his enemies might still take place. But since his attempt to follow Jesus is a half-hearted, doubt-ridden venture, furtive and full of fear, he falls deeper than the others, who at

Figure 131. Peter and the servant girl

129

least had no occasion to deny Jesus explicitly. Because his faith was deep, but not deep enough, the worst happened to him that can happen to one whom faith had inspired but a short time before: he trembles for his miserable life. And it is entirely credible that this terrifying experience should have brought about another swing of the pendulum—this time in the opposite direction and far stronger. Despair and remorse following his desperate failure prepared him for the visions which contributed decisively to the constitution of Christianity. It is only through this experience that the significance of Christ's coming and Passion is revealed to him.

And it is through the gospel narrative of this experience, Auerbach continues, that we perceive the revolution effected by Christianity in the thinking of the ancient world. A classical author would have treated the remorse of a peasant as a joke. Christianity discerned a tragedy.

Figure 132. A. D. Thomas. Indian treatment

Figure 133. Francisco José Goya.
Peter's remorse

18
TRIALS

ONTIUS PILATE, THE ROMAN
governor of Judea, had the final authority in the case of Jesus. But
first came trials before the Jewish authorities, the high priests
Annas and Caiaphas. The latter asked Jesus whether he was the
Christ, the Son of God. Jesus replied, "I am." Caiaphas then tore
his clothes. This was blasphemy, punishable by death according to
Jewish law. John's gospel tells us that the Sanhedrin lacked authority
to pronounce the sentence of death. Yet Stephen was later stoned
without Roman authority. Perhaps the Jews were allowed to stone

but not to crucify. At any rate, after the hearings before the priests, Jesus was sent to Pontius Pilate.

Blasphemy of Israel's God was not a crime of which the Roman government would take cognizance. The offense must be political subversion, and this charge was plausible because on Palm Sunday Jesus had been hailed as king. Jesus told Pilate his kingdom was not of this world. Pilate was persuaded, but the mob was clamorous. Pilate glimpsed a way out of his dilemma by delegating the case to Herod (not Herod the Great), the Jewish tetrarch of Galilee, who happened to be in Jerusalem. This Herod was the one who had executed John the Baptist. Herod was curious to see Jesus and have him work one of his reputed miracles, but Jesus did not work miracles on demand. Herod sent him back to Pilate.

Pilate's dilemma was increased by a dream in which his wife told him she had been greatly troubled lest injustice be done to "this righteous man." The accusers brought a new charge. Jesus had declared himself to be the Son of God. John's gospel says, "When Pilate heard these words, he was the more afraid." Why should he have been? This was a religious offense which did not fall under his jurisdiction. Luther observed that the Romans believed that the gods appeared in human guise. So perhaps Pilate did wonder whether Jesus might be Jupiter or Mercury.

A way out occurred to Pilate. The Roman government in order to curry favor with the Jews would customarily release a prisoner at the time of the Passover. We have no evidence of this custom apart from the New Testament, but then there are many events in antiquity for which there is no more than a single witness. Pilate now suggested, half mockingly, that he release "the King of the Jews." But the mob shouted, "Not this man but Barabbas." This Barabbas was a revolutionary, who in an insurrection had committed murder. Pilate then brought Jesus before the crowd, wearing a crown of thorns and a purple robe given to him in

Figure 134. Flagellation

Figure 135. Crown of thorns

133

mockery by the soldiers. Pilate said, "Here is the man." In Latin this is *ecce homo,* a phrase often used for this scene as a title for pictures and books. (The older English translation was "behold the man.") The gospel reads, "When the chief priests and officers saw him, they cried out, 'Crucify him! Crucify him!'"

We may wonder why there should have been such clamor to make away with Jesus on Thursday, whereas he had been hailed with hosannas on Sunday. Of course, those who cried "crucify" may not have been the same persons who had cried "hosanna." But still, early in the week, the rulers hesitated to put Jesus out of the way for fear of the people, and now Pilate hesitated to release him for fear of the people. There had obviously been a great reversal of feeling. The most obvious explanation is that on Sunday the expectation was widespread that Jesus was the Messiah who would call down legions of angels and drive out the Romans. The cleansing of the temple may have seemed to have been the hour, but after that there were no legions of angels. Jesus did nothing more dramatic than sit in the temple and teach. Be done with him then. Choose Barabbas, a Zealot fighting Rome.

Pilate made further efforts at release. The accusers said, "If you release this man you are not Caesar's friend; everyone who makes himself a king sets himself against Caesar." Pilate asked, "Shall I crucify your king?" They answered, "We have no king but Caesar." Pilate wilted. He might have pointed out that if he released Barabbas, he would also not be Caesar's friend, but then Barabbas was not accused of trying to make himself a king.

In the course of the trials there were repeated instances of abuse and mockery. Pilate ordered Jesus, though uncondemned, to be scourged. In these several instances he was dressed in the purple robe of royalty and given a crown of thorns. A reed was placed in his hand as a sceptre. Some of the mockers bowed in homage. He was blindfolded and struck and taunted to tell who did it.

Figure 136. Matthias Grünewald.
Blind-folding

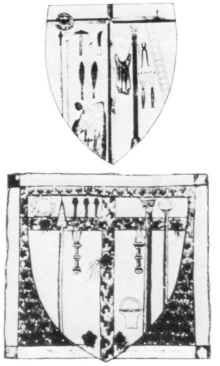

Figure 137. *Arma Christi*

In the artistic representations all of these incidents together, with some from the cross, were combined as to the instruments employed. These instruments were called the *arma Christi*, meaning "the arms of Christ," in the sense of armaments. They are the weapons by which in suffering he had conquered. The separate items were grouped within the frame of a shield and thus became a coat of arms for Christ.

We find in the various examples now one, now another of the following: the purple robe or the seamless robe of the crucifixion, the crown of thorns, the scourge and flail, a club with spikes, the reed of mockery, the pillar to which Jesus was bound for the scourging, and the thong with which he was bound. One grouping from the crucifixion depicts the nails, a hammer and pliers for removing the nails, the lance, the sponge, and the dice thrown by the soldiers. The cock that crowed at Peter's denial occasionally appeared. Those given here are arranged within a heraldic shield. Such designs were used in manuals of devotion. In Figure 138, the crown of thorns pressed into the Savior's scalp in derision was portrayed as the diadem of the King of Kings. Christ in repose after the scourging was often depicted as the Man of Sorrows. Dürer has combined the Christ resting after the flagellation with the Christ crucified showing the nail prints. The portrayal in Luther's Bible avoids this conflation.

Figure 138. Diadem of thorns

Figure 139. Albrecht Dürer. Man of Sorrows

All of the trials—before Annas, Caiaphas, Herod, and Pilate—have received artistic treatment. The one most appealing to the artists was the one before Caiaphas in which he tore his vest. The trial before Pilate has received the most frequent treatment. But his wife has received less notice (male chauvinism?) than Barabbas. She does appear in the fifteenth century with a tiny black devil near her head (Figure 142). Surely this midget should have been placed next to Pilate, but there was not enough room between the heads of husband and wife. (Note here that Pilate's washing of his hands is a part of the same scene.) In the sixteenth century,

Figure 140. Man of Sorrows from Luther's Bible

Figure 141. Caiaphas rends his garment

Figure 142. Pilate's wife with Pilate washing his hands (15th century)

Figure 144. Ralph Coleman.
Before Pilate (20th century)

Figure 143. Albrecht Dürer (16th century)

Dürer introduced Pilate's wife into the *Ecce Homo* scene. If she had appeared as Dürer depicts, might not Pilate have feared to offend her more than Caesar? There is a modern depiction in which Pilate is a bull-necked brute, his wife a gentle lass who would normally conquer by eloquence and tears.

Barabbas was introduced in early *Ecce Homo* scenes. In the Rossano gospel of the first part of the sixth century, we see him before Pilate along with Christ. Barabbas is held by a guard. Chains hold his hands and apparently his feet, and a chain goes from his neck to the person in front of him. Christ is free and wears a halo. In Figure 146, the head of Barabbas is seen through a grate in the prison window. But the other by Rembrandt places him on the balcony along with Christ and Pilate.

Figure 145. Barabbas chained

Figure 146. Jörg Ratgeb.
Barabbas in prison

Figure 147. Rembrandt van Rijn.
Barabbas on the balcony (1655)

Figure 148. Quentin Massys.
The rabble on the balcony

Figure 149. Antonio Ciseri.
Pilate faces the mob

One of the most frightful portrayals of the howling mob is by
Quentin Massys, who puts some of the rabble on the balcony.
Barabbas is not in this work, nor is he in an unusual modern depiction where Christ stands with his back to us a little left of center.
In this same picture, Pilate leans over the balustrade addressing the
mob below; his left hand points backwards at Christ. His wife is in
the right foreground.

Figure 150. Hans Hirtz.
Mary and John on the way to the cross

Figure 151. E. Koch.
The collapse on the way to the cross

The way of Christ to Calvary, called the Via Dolorosa, is sometimes depicted with a few figures, sometimes with a crowd. Luke says "there followed a great multitude." Since Mary and John were at the cross, they are assumed to have traveled the road to Golgotha. They appear in Figure 150. Veronica and her napkin are often shown.

The collapse of Christ beneath the cross is poignantly shown by a German artist in the East Zone after World War II. Christ has fallen. The throng goes heedlessly on. Historically, Christ did not carry the cross after the collapse but was replaced by Simon of Cyrene, who was impressed for the service. We have already noticed that the artist Cranach gave his own features to Simon.

A realistic representation of the placing of Christ upon the cross involved laying the cross upon the ground, nailing his hands and feet and then raising the cross by ropes to an upright position and sinking it into a socket in the rock (Figure 152). Another depiction shows Christ climbing a ladder to be affixed to the cross already in position. For all the lack of historical realism, there is here, a profound idea. The artist was no doubt thinking of the words in John's gospel: "For this purpose I have come to this hour." Thus, Christ is committed to the fulfillment of his destiny. God had chosen a moment in time to incarnate himself uniquely in a man who must die to release others from the bondage of sin. But if this was needful, was it not necessary that the Son of Man should be betrayed by Judas, condemned by Caiaphas, and crucified by Pilate? And if they were playing necessary roles in a drama of redemption, are they to be blamed? Here is an enigma which has and will trouble the ages.

Figure 152. Stecher. Erecting the cross

Figure 153. Christ mounts the cross

19
CRUCIFIXION

HE CRUCIFIXION HAS RECEIVED
greater representation in art than any other event or aspect of the
life of Christ. This, at any rate, is true for the West, where the
emphasis has been on the forgiveness of sins through the sacrificial
death of Christ. In the East, the stress has been on the restoration of
fallen man. "God became man in order that man might become
God." The Christian did not, of course, become the Lord of all the
universe, but rather a new creature, a participant of the divine
nature. The important event, then, was the incarnation, and the
icons portrayed the Virgin in whose womb the Word became flesh
as the Mother of God.

Yet the crucifix entered rather late into Christian art even in
the West. Prior to Constantine the fathers of the Church would

Figure 154. The cross and the wreath

allow no more than an anchor on a seal as a symbol of the cross. The great change came with Constantine who had a vision of the cross. We do not know what was already in his mind to have had such a vision. We do know that during his time, Christians began to have the cross carved on their tombs.

Figure 154 is not a crucifix, but a cross without the body of Christ. Two guards are beneath the arms, one of them asleep. Above the cross is a wreath of laurel; doves on the arms of the cross are pecking at its berries. Such a wreath was the award given to the winner in the Greek games. Here it signifies the victory of Christ over death. Within the circle is the monogram of Christ. Thus, we have combined the symbols of the passion and the resurrection.

A depiction of Christ on the cross is not found until the middle of the fourth century. He is shown naked with arms of exaggerated length. The feet rest on a pedestal. On each side are six apostles. The writing is in mirror script, because this is a seal for stamping in wax. The name *Jesus* is transliterated as *E á su* (*a* as in *ale*). The *X*, our *Ch*, is to our right of the cross. On the other side we have, in our alphabet, *REST*, and at the very bottom, the letters *OS*. The name *Christ* is thus given as *Chrestos*. Is the little animal below there, the ass on which Jesus rode into Jerusalem? This seal has been assumed to date from the time before Constantine, but that is not likely because Christ has a halo and no other example is known of a halo before A.D. 340. The halo, also called a nimbus, was taken over from the aureole about the head of a pagan god.

Figure 155. Earliest depiction of Christ on the cross

Figure 156. Crucifix (ca. 400)

Figure 156, an ivory carving now in the British Museum, is from the fifth century. The title above the head of Christ, *Rex Jud.*, is Latin for "King of the Jews." Christ is alive. His eyes are open. The arms are horizontal; the body, vertical. The feet appear to have no support. The chin is beardless. There is no halo. The two figures on the left are Mary and John. The figure on the other side may be the soldier who pierced Christ's body, though he appears to be about to strike a blow. On the far left, Judas is hanging himself. The thirty pieces of silver spill out at his feet. On a branch of the tree above a dove is feeding her fledglings.

A century later we have a fuller depiction from Syria. The inscription above the cross is in Syriac. The word *melka*, meaning "king," is clearly legible. Christ is bearded as in the Syrian tradition. He is given a halo. The feet appear to be held up only by nails. Whether he is strapped as well as nailed, like the two thieves, is not clear since he is draped. The reason for draping cannot have been an objection to the nude as such, because the thieves are nearly naked. Clothing Christ may have been due to the influence of the Monophysites (the name is from the Greek words meaning "one

Figure 157. Crucifix (ca. 500)

Figure 158. Crucifix with loincloth at Rome

nature"), who held that Christ had only a divine nature and that to portray this as naked would be to dishonor.

The details of this picture are taken chiefly from John's gospel, which relates that beneath the cross stood the haloed Mary, the Mother of Jesus, and the disciple whom Jesus loved, commonly assumed to have been John. They are here on the far left. On the far right are three Marys—Mary, the Mother of Jesus without halo; Mary, the wife of Cleophas; and Mary Magdalene. Consequently, in this depiction, the Mother of Jesus appears twice.

While Jesus was yet alive, a soldier offered him a sponge soaked in vinegar to dull his pain. In legend he was called Stephanos, but is not named here. After Jesus was dead, another soldier pierced his side with a spear. He was called Longinus, here spelled *Loginos*.

Since Mark's gospel tells us that during the crucifixion "there was darkness over all the land" for three hours, the sun and the moon commonly appear in crucifixion scenes as participants in the drama. Here, the moon has a face. The soldiers, being loathe to cut up the seamless robe of Jesus, cast lots—here dice—for possession.

There is a rather similar treatment on the door of St. Sabina at Rome, except that in this instance Christ is not draped. At first there was objection to his near nudity. But in time, both in the East and the West, the type with only the loincloth prevailed. The reason may have been historical realism. Criminals were not crucified in their clothes.

In the Romanesque period in the West, Christ "the crucified"

Figure 159. Villard de Honnecourt. The dead Christ on the cross

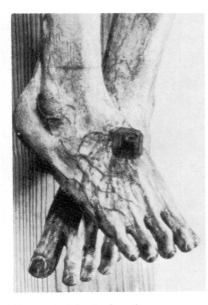

Figure 160. The single nail

was not as common as Christ "the judge of all the world." But occasionally in the tenth century and more commonly in the twelfth century and thereafter, the European mind was obsessed by a sense of guilt to be expunged through the sacrificial death of Christ. The measure of his sacrifice was depicted by showing him dead upon the cross (Figure 159). The head fell over on the right shoulder. The arms sagged. The legs were crossed and the feet held by a single nail (Figure 160). The knees were raised and the whole body assumed the shape of the letter *S*, betokening the utter lassitude after the agony of death. At the foot was the skull of Adam, whose corruption of the human race was rectified by the suffering of Christ.

In the same period there were, however, other types. One was the eucharistic Christ, which had to be alive in order that the blood might flow from the wounds. In Figure 161, three little angels, one using both hands, are catching the blood in chalices for sacramental use. The skull of Adam is again below. Figure 162 is remarkable because in the background is a picture of a pagan sacrifice. The artist was correct in sensing a pagan antecedent to the devotion of the Holy Blood. Still, in the Renaissance, the belief continued that, as the Bible said (Gen. 9:4), the soul is in the blood. By drinking the blood of a man or an animal, one imbibed his strength, and by being bathed in the blood of an animal one could imbibe the divine power by which he was filled. The devotee would be placed in a pit under a grate. A bull or a goat would be killed above and the blood would bespatter the initiate.

Such rites come to mind when one looks at Bernini's crucifixion from the period of the Counter-Reformation. The blood flows in streams from the wounded hands. Protestants, no less, have talked of being "washed in the blood of the Lamb," and have sung, "There is a fountain filled with blood drawn from Emmanuel's veins." And today I even see young people waltzing up to the altar singing, "Eat his body, drink his blood."

Figure 161. Eucharistic crucifix

Figure 162. Giovanni Bellini. Crucifix
and pagan sacrifice

Figure 163. From G. L. Bernini's
"Fountain filled with blood"

149

Figure 164. The crucifix consoling St. Bernard

The piety of the Cistercians and Franciscans introduced a different style. Both stressed the infinite love and tenderness of Christ. A manuscript from a Cistercian abbey shows the body of Christ attached to the cross only by one nail through the feet. The crucifix leans forward and the arms are ready to embrace St. Bernard. The drawing does not, however, date from the time of the saint since Christ wears the crown of thorns which does not appear on the crucifix until the thirteenth century. Franciscan piety in that century led also to a diminished emphasis on the physical suffering

Figure 165. School of Giotto. "Weep not for me"

Figure 166. Christ comforted by Lady Poverty

of Christ. There is a crucifixion by the School of Giotto in which the agony is rather in the faces of Mary and John than of Christ, who seems almost to be saying, as on another occasion, "Daughters of Jerusalem, weep not for me." There are even examples in which the Lady Poverty comforts Christ upon the cross (Figure 166).

The portrayals just mentioned are French and Italian. The German depictions during the same period were marked by greater

Figure 167. German crucifix with blood on the legs

Figure 168. Hans Holbein. Christ of agony

Figure 169. Matthias Grünewald.
Unutterable desolation

realism of physical pain. Figure 167, for example, shows drops of blood standing out on arms and legs. A sketch by Holbein is in the same tradition, his "dead Christ" is utterly livid. One must beware, however, of treating such realism as exclusively German. After the Black Death in 1348, all of Europe suffered a preoccupation with death. The most popular books after the introduction of printing were called *The Art of Dying*.

Sepulchral monuments were macabre. There is a tomb in the St. Elizabeth's church at Marburg on which lies a sculptured corpse with entrails protruding and worms at work. Such a background helps one to approach the crucifixion of Grünewald, hailed by some as the greatest crucifixion ever painted. It is distinctive in the lividness of the hues, in the gnarled fingers extending above the arms of the cross, and in the intense agony of the faces of Mary and John. On the right John the Baptist points with elongated finger to the Lamb of God that takes away the sins of the world.

But if the Germans leaned to the gruesome, the Spaniards passed to the macabre. The most blood-reeking crucifixes and

Figure 170. Mexican.
Blood-reeking crown of thorns

Figure 171. Ignacio Zuloaga.
Flagellation

Figure 173. Miracle of the diverted bull

Figure 172. Pablo Picasso.
Christ the matador

Figure 174. Pablo Picasso. Bones on the cross

pictures of Christ crowned with thorns come from Spain and Mexico. These portrayals were not an outgrowth of the German type, but appear to have arisen from the intense piety of the Counter-Reformation. Two other phenomena peculiarly Spanish may throw light on the ethos of these crucifixes. The first is flagellation. The Spanish painter of the nineteenth century, Zuloaga, depicts the usage still in vogue. Below a crucifix crouches a penitent with back bare to be lashed to shreds. The second is the bullfight. In antiquity, the bull was a sacred animal the shedding of whose blood increased fertility, and bathing in whose blood conveyed power to man. How easily such notions could be transferred to the blood of Christ! The Church tried frequently to suppress the paganism, but popular piety triumphed and the canonization of St. Teresa in 1622 was celebrated with a bullfight.

Picasso picked up the ancient theme when he portrayed Christ as the matador on the cross. Was he reworking an earlier drawing in which, while matador and horse lay prone, the crucifix with a cape saved their lives by diverting the bull? Picasso certainly did not believe it, for he reached the ultimate of the impotence of Christ in a drawing of the cross, bearing nothing more than an agglomeration of bones. Another artist, steeped in the Mexican tradition, has placed the bull on the cross being crucified by the matador. This harks back to the sacrifice of the bull. In these three—crucifixion, flagellation, and the bullfight—the common element is the courting of death. Is this penitential? Is it masochistic? Is it a sublimation of the martial?

A curious detail is, that to facilitate removal for processions, crucifixes of the fourteenth century in south Germany were supplied with detachable arms.

If all of the crucifixes thus far described seem inadequate and some perverse, what would be an ideal depiction? First of all, it must show pain. The uniqueness of Christianity is that, of all religions, it squarely confronts the hideousness of sin and the

Figure 175. The bull on the cross

Figure 176. Detachable arms of the crucifix

155

Figure 177. Rembrandt van Rijn.
Eli! Eli! (My God! My God!)

Figure 178. William Blake.
Darkness on the face of the land

Figure 179. Georges Rouault. Infinite sadness

poignancy of tragedy to be swallowed up in victory. The victory is the greater because the sufferings are real. The theme in a recent hymn of God dancing on the cross is inappropriate. Crucifixion is no dance. But the pain is not so much that of the body as of the spirit. Christ had been rejected by the leaders of his people, betrayed by Judas, denied by Peter, abandoned by his disciples. The very *sun* had withdrawn its light. And Jesus cried, "My God! My God! Why hast thou forsaken me?" To convey the feeling of that cry, Christ must be shown alive. And so it is for the other words upon the cross; the comfort to the penitent thief, the prayer of forgiveness for the brutal soldiers, the concern for the mother, the acquiescence in the will of God.

Spiritual suffering calls for a live Christ. None other can convey the import of the cry "My God! My God! Why hast thou forsaken me?" Rembrandt has done it. Whether he was anticipated, I am not sure. There were earlier portrayals interpreted in this sense because the mouth is open. But the mouth can sag in death. The eyes also must be open. In the Rembrandt there is a still more indicative feature. The muscles of the neck are taut.

Blake has conveyed the sense of the eclipse during the crucifixion by using white lines on a totally black background. Rouault's "Man of Sorrows" betokens the infinite sadness of him on whom was laid "the iniquities of us all." Chagall, showing Jews in flight around the crucifix, makes it the symbol of the never ending suffering of his people.

Figure 180. Marc Chagall. The eternal Jew

20
DEPOSITION FROM THE CROSS AND PIETÀ

EPOSITION OF THE BODY of Christ from the cross provided an opportunity to recognize two lesser disciples: Nicodemus, who had visited Jesus only by night and now brought aloes and myrrh to anoint the body, and Joseph of **Arimathea**, a secret disciple who secured permission from Pilate to remove the body. In earlier depictions these two are shown letting down the body with great tenderness. But our age is so chary of

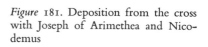

Figure 181. Deposition from the cross with Joseph of Arimethea and Nicodemus

Figure 182. Ethiopian depiction

159

Figure 183. From Desvallières's deposition

Figure 184. Wide Silva. Ceylonese depiction

Figure 185. Hans Holbein. The dead Christ

sentimentality that the French artist, Desvallières has given a ghastly rendition which may well be closer to historical reality. The body of Christ, lowered by ropes, is dangling midway above the swooning Mary. One barely sees the hand of Joseph of Arimathea.

Depictions are also frequent of the dead body awaiting entombment. I have seen none more ghastly than that by Holbein with its livid hues. Some discern here the end of the Middle Ages, for Holbein next went to England to paint the vibrant Tudor nobility. Dead Christs did not sell anymore. The Renaissance had triumphed. Scarcely! This is an exaggeration. The piety of the cross was not extinguished. But there may have been a transition in Holbein himself.

The portrayal of Mary holding the dead Christ in her arms is called a *pietà*. There are as many varieties in the mode of depiction as in the case of the crucifixion. An example from the fifteenth century still has the quaintness of the medieval book illustration. Southern Germany, during the same general period, had many examples of unsurpassed ugliness. One wonders how any could derive comfort from the sight of such an excruciating figure, but the observation has been well made that one intoxicated with religion may prefer the ugly. Beauty, especially the beauty of the human body, brings the holy too near. There are many other treatments marked by great tenderness. Two examples given here are from Italy: one by Giovanni Bellini, the other by Michelangelo. The latter was dictated by the Neoplatonic ideal of composure. Mary's face is not racked by grief, but marked by a pensive melancholy.

Figure 186. Fifteenth-century *pietà*

Figure 187. "No comeliness"

Figure 189. Michelangelo Buonarroti. The pensive Mary

Figure 188. Giovanni Bellini. Pietà

Figure 190. Rubbed-out pietà

The era of persecution in Japan of the seventeenth century has bequeathed to us a pietà in which the features have been rubbed away, because the government called upon the villagers to prove their dissociation from the faith by rubbing their feet on bronze plaques of Christ. A few have survived. The features are effaced but the outline remains of the ineffaceable Christ.

21
RESURRECTION

ESURRECTION IS very surely the cardinal event in Christian history, and one may wonder whether Christianity could ever have become a world religion without it. Possibly it might. Buddhism, Hinduism, and Islam are world religions without resurrections. Mani in Persia was crucified and, though he did not rise again, his religion spread widely in the Roman empire. St. Augustine was an adherent at one time. But, in competition with the dying and rising of the mystery religions, Christianity might never have survived without a similar and weightier counterclaim. The mystery gods were personifications of nature, gods of fertility. They promised a blessed immortality to their devotees through identification with nature's forces. Christianity offered a greater assurance, because Jesus was not a personification but a person, who by dying and rising gave men the confidence that through him and also for them, "death was swallowed up in victory."

Figure 191. Jonah dancing above the waves

Since the resurrection was crucial for Christian faith, one marvels that it received no pictorial representation for a thousand years. This is not to say that there was no intimation in art, but only that direct depiction of Christ emerging from the tomb does not come for a millennium. The reason may have been reluctance to portray the divine. The theme of resurrection was, however, conveyed in other ways: by symbol—the laurel wreath above the cross; by typology, the analogy of deliverances from death in the Old Testament—Noah coming from the ark, Daniel from the den of lions, Jonah from the whale. (See him in Figure 191 disporting himself above the waves.)

In addition the resurrection was indicated by depiction of occurrences possible only because preceded by the resurrection; the empty tomb, the ascension, the descent to hell, and various appearances. The ascension certainly presupposed the resurrection, unless indeed the ascension *was* the resurrection. Some so regarded it. Paul may have done so. He counted himself a witness to the resurrection but gave no tangible details of contact with the risen Christ. The accounts of the encounters on the road to Damascus with Jesus by sight and sound are all in the Book of Acts. Paul said only, "When God was pleased to reveal his Son to me" (Galatians 1:16).

Figure 192. Ascension and resurrection

The resurrection, practically as the ascension, is portrayed in a sculpture from Gaul, presumably about the year 400. Figure 192 shows a mausoleum on which someone leans, weeping. Above, there is a tree with birds pecking at the fruit—an extraneous detail to fill up space. Below on the right are three women, plainly those who, on Easter morning, came to the tomb. A young man beside the tomb is addressing them. He must be the angel, though as yet without wings. At the right on the top is the (haloed) Christ, climbing up a cliff—or is it a bank of clouds? Beneath him are the watchers at the tomb, one asleep, the other startled. From above, the hand of God reaches down to assist the ascent. The Church never forgot that the resurrection was a work of God. The central theme of this picture is the ascension. The resurrection, if at all distinct, is to be inferred from the women, the angel, and the watchers.

Throughout the Middle Ages the women at the tomb signalized the resurrection. Sometimes there are three, sometimes two. In the fresco of the Dura baptistry we recall that they were five. They

Figure 193. Bartolomeo Schedoni. The three Marys

are called "the three Marys," though the designation is not accurate. The gospels give different lists of names. In Mark we have Mary Magdalene, Mary the mother of James, and Salome. Since Jesus had a brother James, the inference was that Jesus' mother was also the mother of James; however, that is an odd way to speak of the mother of the Lord. Luke has Joanna instead of Salome. Matthew says Mary Magdalene and "the other Mary." Which other Mary? John has only Mary Magdalene. These differences are of course inconsequential. They show how little the evangelists were concerned about consistency of detail, which may be the result of collusion. Discrepancies are the proof of independence and honesty. The three Marys continued to be portrayed long after depictions of the actual resurrection had been introduced. Figure 193 is an example from the seventeenth century.

Another scene requiring an antecedent resurrection was "the harrowing of hell," to use the expression which gained currency in England. It meant the "descent into hell," as phrased in the Apostles' Creed. This creed did not receive its definitive form until the ninth century, though a reference to the descent into hell is found in the fourth century. "Hell," as a matter of fact, is not the correct word to use. It should be Hades. Hell was a place of torment; Hades, a place of detention where the worthies of the Old Testament were confined until Christ's coming.

There was some warrant in the New Testament for the assumption that Christ went down into Hades to effect the deliverance of the detained. Matthew's gospel tells us that during the crucifixion "the earth shook, and the rocks were split; the tombs also opened, and many bodies of the saints who had fallen asleep were raised, and coming out of the tombs after his resurrection they went into the holy city and appeared to many" (Matthew 27:51-53). That Christ had delivered them was inferred from 1 Peter 3:19, which says that Christ "preached to the spirits in prison." But the details depicted in the pictures are derived from the apocryphal Gospel of Nicodemus. The term *apocryphal* is applied to those early Christian gospels and acts of apostles that were allowed to be read in the churches but were not included in the Scripture. There is no greater evidence of the inspiration of the Scriptures than the inspired judgment of the early Church that the apocryphal writings were not inspired.

Here is a passage from the Gospel of Nicodemus. Not only Satan but Hell and Hades are personified. Satan tells Hell that Christ is coming. Hell replies:

"If it be he that by the word of his command alone made Lazarus, which was four days dead, to fly out of my bosom like an eagle, then he is not a man in his manhood, but God in his majesty. I beseech thee, bring him not unto me." Satan saith to him: "Notwithstanding, make thyself ready, fear not: for already he hangeth upon a cross, and I can do no other." Then Hell spake thus unto Satan: "If then, thou canst do no other, lo thy destruction draweth near, and I shall at last be cast down and remain without honor; but thou wilt be tormented under my dominion."

Then came the voice of the Son of the most high Father, as the voice of a great thunder, saying: "Lift up, O princes, your gates, and be ye lifted up, ye everlasting doors, and the King of glory shall come in." Then Satan and Hell cried out, saying: "Who is this King of Glory?" And it was answered them by the Lord's voice: "The Lord strong and mighty, the Lord mighty in battle." . . . And lo, suddenly Hell did quake, and the gates of death and the locks were broken small, and the bars of iron broken, and fell to the ground, and all things were laid open. And Satan remained in the midst and stood put to confusion and cast down, and bound with a fetter about his feet. And behold, the Lord Jesus Christ coming in the glory of the light of the height, in meekness, great and yet humble, bearing a chain in his hands, bound therewith the neck of Satan, and also, binding his hands behind his back, cast him backward into Tartarus, and set his holy foot upon his throat. . . And the Lord set his cross

169

in the midst of hell, which is the sign of victory: and it shall remain there forever.

The general release follows. And here endeth the reading from the Gospel of Nicodemus.

In the first of our illustrations of this theme, Christ is knocking open the door of hell with his foot. Figure 195, dating from the fourteenth century, shows the throng of the liberated. Adam comes first. Behind him with the lamb is Abel. Noah has a miniature of his ark with a hole in the roof, perhaps for the escape of the dove. David, "the sweet singer of Israel," has a scroll with musical notation, and Moses has something from the Law.

Figure 194. Knocking open the gate of Hades

Figure 195. Release of the spirits in prison

Figure 196. Albrecht Dürer.
The release and the penitent thief

In the sixteenth century, we have a copperplate by Dürer in which Christ reaches down to pull up Adam. Behind Christ is a tall man carrying a large cross. He is the penitent thief who had taken his cross along with him; this alone insured his entrance to paradise. Dürer has an assembly of devils about and above Adam, showing bats' wings, boars' snouts, rams' horns, vultures' beaks, and snakes' necks. Along with all these, plus dragons and apes, there are sometimes human forms with expressions more rebellious and vile than those of the beasts. Naturally the animals that prey upon man are regarded as demonic, yet may there not also be the recognition that many of the anti-social acts of man are survivals from an animal heritage? But when man appears more repulsive than the beast, one realizes that demonism with advance in intelligence takes on more sinister forms.

Christ of course routs them all. "He treads upon the lion and the adder, the young lion and the serpent he tramples under foot" (Psalm 91:13). See him in a portrayal from the thirteenth century, trampling on a serpentine demon.

The image of Christ—the valiant trampling on his foe—appealed to the Nordic hosts invading the old Roman empire. These were warlike folk who often militarized the gospel. The first Christian poem in the old Germanic tongue glorified Peter precisely because he did cut off the high priest's servant's ear:

Then boiled with wrath
The swift sword wielder,
Simon Peter,
Speechless he,
Grieved his heart
That any sought
To bind his Master,
Grim the knight faced
Boldly the servants,
Shielding his Suzerain,
Not craven his heart,
Lightening swift
Unsheathed his sword,
Strode to the first foe,
Smote a strong stroke,
Clave with the sharp blade,
On the right side
The ear of Malchus.

Figure 197. Trampling on the demon

The saints were militarized and became the heavenly champions of the peoples: George for England, Andrew for Scotland, David for Wales, James for Spain, Denis for France. Christ himself was depicted leading the crusading host (Figure 198). In his mouth is the sword described in the Apocalypse, while God the Father in the upper left corner, looking younger than the Son, raises a hand in blessing.

Figure 198. Christ the crusader

173

Figure 199. The general resurrection

Figure 200. Earliest depiction of Christ stepping from the tomb

But to return. The ascension, the empty tomb, and the harrowing of hell were the artistic intimations of the resurrection. Depictions of the general resurrection of the dead preceded those of Christ rising out of the tomb by some two hundred years. The example here of the general resurrection is not the earliest and dates from about the year 1000. On the fourth row, the man with the beard and the bib is Adam. Just below him, holding the lid of the coffin, is Eve. The first actual depiction of Christ stepping out of the tomb, a plain box of a coffin, dates from around 1020. The beast glowering at Christ is not a demon but the lion of Saint Mark. The inscription below in Latin says "Leo [the lion] the mighty leaps over the the boundaries of death."

175

Figure 201. Meister Franke.
A cautious emergence

Figure 202. Peter Paul Rubens.
A tumultuous emergence

Figure 203. The waltzing Christ

Once the reluctance to portray Christ rising from the tomb had been overcome, portrayals began to abound. They vary little in type, though one may contrast a fifteenth-century painting in which Christ with stealth steps gingerly out of the sarcophagus lest he wake the watchers, with one by Rubens in the seventeenth century which shows him striding forth tumultuously, sweeping all before him. Some artists went even further and had him waltzing through the empyrean (Figure 203). Here the figure of the dance of God is appropriate. The resurrection and ascension are blended in an Indonesian treatment. Grünewald achieves a dramatic effect by setting the resurrection against a midnight sky.

These differences are trifling. The anomaly is that all of these depictions coincide in time with the representations of Christ dead

Figure 205. Matthias Grünewald.
Resurrection at midnight

Figure 204. Wajan Turun.
Resurrection as ascension in Indonesia

on the cross. Why, in the same century, should we have a Christ in utter languor, slumped over the bars of the cross and a Christ, vibrant and aggressive, striding from the tomb? Is the reason precisely to point up the contrast? The miracle of the resurrection is enhanced by showing that it is a real resurrection from a genuine death.

Both modes involve a materializing of the faith. The crucifixion is shown with ghastly realism. This is a real physical body with stigmata in hands and feet and lacerations of the torso. The risen Christ, though able to vanish and pass through a door (Figure 206), was tangible enough for Thomas to be invited to put his hand into the wound and corporeal enough to eat a fish. There was certainly a craving for the tangible. We have already noted the depiction of the instruments of Christ's passion in the manuals of devotion. But more than that, these instruments were believed to have been actually discovered. St. Helena, the mother of Constantine, had located the holy cross. Excavation in Jerusalem had unearthed three crosses. The one that brought a corpse to life was the cross of Christ. The nails also were found. Helena sent them to Constantine, who put one in his helmet and used one for the bit of his horse. The crusaders returning from the Holy Land brought back bags of relics. The Pope was able to give the German emperor the inscription over the cross and distributed thorns from the crown of thorns to many of the crowned heads of Europe. The relics had religious significance. They wrought miracles thereby proving their own authenticity and the authenticity of the events.

Associated with the relics were indulgences, which also began in this period. The vendor would begin by displaying the relics of the saints whose superfluous merits were to be transferred to subscribers. The very theory of indulgences meant a materializing of the vices and the virtues which were treated quantitatively, subject

Figure 206. Through the closed door.

to addition and subtraction.

Coincidently, however, there were countercurrents. Gothic architecture in time converted the material into the immaterial. At first the masons used material stone to scale the battlements of heaven. The heights achieved were astonishing. The cathedral of Chartres equals the elevation of a skyscraper of thirty stories, and that of Strasbourg rises to forty stories. But limits to height were discovered in the course of repeated failures. A historian of cathedrals has remarked that the question to put to a guide is, "When did the tower fall?" That of Mont St. Michel collapsed twice. Then, when the greatest height consonant with stability had been reached, the architect sought to create the illusion of elevation. The employment of flying buttresses eliminated the massive walls of the Romanesque and made possible slender pillars, which, in turn, were carved in the form of a cluster of still more slender shafts reaching to infinity. The sculptured forms standing in their niches were elongated: the neck, the arms, and the legs seemed not to be in repose but leaping upwards. Stone was made to belie its very nature, so that it seemed to soar. The material had become the immaterial.

This was true in another way, arising from God's descent in response to man's ascent. Such language is of course figurative, but since fiery eruptions belch from below and light streams down from above, aspiration has always been called ascent and the divine response, descent. The great symbol here is light. The Gothic cathedrals were inundated by light. The walls, superfluous between the buttresses, were filled with glass—not clear cold glass, but ruby, crimson, azure, and indigo, as golden as the sun, opalescent, sparkling like jewels, twinkling like stars, changing hourly from the dazzle of dawn to the glow of dusk. The light in manifold hues falling on the cold dead stone made a living tapestry of the pavement. The material had again become the immaterial.

Such were the contrasts. Were they perhaps simply an embodiment of the stresses of the time? The twelfth century has been called a "renaissance before the Renaissance." Every renaissance is marked by stresses. The balance of thrust and counterthrust was the very principle of the Gothic, and this not only with respect to the structure, but also to the themes. The capitals of the columns and the borders of the windows set forth the glory of creation with accurate delineations of the flowers and the foliage of the burgeoning spring; the waterspouts took the form of leering gargoyles, sardonic minions of the Prince of Darkness. The rood bore the crucified. The tympanum exhibited the judge of all the world, the windows displayed the Lord of life: Christ sagging dead upon the cross and Christ seated at the right hand of God the Father. Equilibrium was found in the concord of opposites.

Now that actual depiction of the rising of Christ had emerged, three scenes of the risen Christ became popular, though to a degree they had appeared earlier. Chief among them were the appearance to Mary Magdalene in the garden, the episode of doubting Thomas, and the disclosure of Christ to the disciples at Emmaus.

In the case of Mary we have the account only in John's gospel, that early in the morning, while it was still dark, Mary Magdalene came to the tomb and, finding the stone rolled away and the body not there, went and told Peter and the beloved disciple. They came

Figure 207. "Touch me not" (10th century)

and made the same observation and went home, but she remained in the garden weeping. Seeing Jesus, and supposing him to be the gardener, she asked him if he had removed the body, and if so, to tell her where. Jesus said to her, "Mary." She answered, "Rabboni," and must have made a gesture of embrace. "Touch me not," he said, "for I am not yet ascended to the Father."

The usual depictions show the scene in daylight, which it may well have been, since the two men had had time to come and go home again. A portrayal from the tenth century is very simple with no touch of symbolism save the halo for Jesus only. In Figure 208, Christ has a crozier and banner but no halo. The most striking piece of symbolism here is that the tree next to Christ is dead, whereas those in the distance are in leaf. This was not an uncommon device for contrasting death and life.

Dürer assumed that the light was just breaking. He gave Christ a spade and a hat rather than a halo. Rembrandt, dispensing with signs and symbols, set the scene before dawn and thus achieved striking contrasts.

Figure 208. Martin Schongauer. "Touch me not" (16th century)

Figure 209. Albrecht Dürer. The gardener

Figure 210. Rembrandt van Rijn. Before dawn

Figure 211. Doubting Thomas (11th century)

The account of "doubting Thomas" is also related only in John's gospel, where we are told that Thomas, being informed by the other disciples of their encounter in his absence with the risen Lord, said he would not believe unless he could put his finger in the nail prints. Then Jesus appeared again to the disciples and told Thomas to do exactly that. Instead, he exclaimed, "My Lord and my God!" Several of the illustrations show him actually inserting his finger into the wound in Christ's side. Others more accurately display rather his emotion. Here are examples, one from the Middle Ages, one from the late sixteenth century. The commentators have always been puzzled why Jesus told Mary not to touch him and told Thomas that he might.

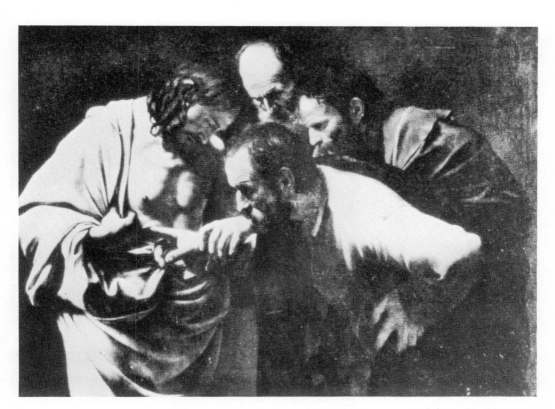

Figure 212. Polidoro da Caravaggio.
Doubting Thomas (1595)

Figure 213. Polidoro da Caravaggio.
His earlier Emmaus

Figure 214. Polidoro da Caravaggio.
His later Emmaus

The disclosure of the risen Christ to two disciples as they journeyed to Emmaus is related in Luke 24:13-32. The disciples did not recognize their companion but afterwards confessed that as they talked, their hearts burned within them. Arriving at the village and sitting at table, "he took the bread and blessed and broke it, and gave it to them. And their eyes were opened and they recognized him: and he vanished from their sight."

Figure 215. Offer of a fish

Note here that in two portrayals of this scene we have an example of how one artist, a bit carried away by the exhilaration of a new technique, was more interested in its display than in the message. Later, this same artist, having matured in his own experience, subordinated craftsmanship to the theme. We have noticed this already in the case of Dürer's two treatments of the Last Supper. Now, for the Emmaus scene, we have a like development in Caravaggio. The earlier depiction is simply breathtaking for the contrasts of light and shade which he inaugurated. At the center of the picture is the hand of Christ. And there the eye remains, entranced by the modelling through highlight and shadow of the fingers and the thumb. The same is true of the leg bones of the chicken on the table, the veins in the leaf, and the rounded contours of the grapes. In his second treatment, the face of Christ, slightly to the left, draws the eye which then shifts to the faces of the host and hostess—solicitous, but unmindful of the wonder.

The appearances in Galilee receive less treatment than those at Jerusalem. We have several examples of the miraculous draft of fishes, of the disciples offering the risen Christ a fish to eat, and of the great commission to "make disciples of all nations" (Matthew 28:19).

One of the strangest and in a way the most modern rendering of Christ's emergence from the tomb is that of Michelangelo in his early years. Christ is bursting from the grave as a young athlete

Figure 216. Great commission

Figure 217. Michelangelo Buonarroti. Christ bursting from the tomb

carrying all before him through his own prowess. The drawing has been described as the most blasphemous of all portrayals.

As Dürer portrayed himself in the role of the Man of Sorrows, and Cranach gave his face to Simon of Cyrene, so Michelangelo injected his spirit into the Christ who bursts the bonds. Here is the tortured genius struggling to capture the beautiful, to encompass the ineffable. Impatient of all the trammels of space and time, he will be master of his destiny.

The spirit of Michelangelo, oscillating between the agony and the ecstasy, came to be chastened till he saw the sculptor's hammer guided by a hand not his own. On the death of Vittoria Colonna, to whose devotional poetry he owed much, he composed this sonnet:

> The sculptor's hammer according to his will
> Gives to the rugged stone a human form.
> The hammer of itself knows not the norm
> And must be guided by the sculptor's skill.
> The hammer forged remains a hammer still.
> There is a power that rides above the storm,
> Beauty alone creates, invests with form,
> Able to recreate and also kill.
> The hammer, if the hand be lifted high,
> Descends with greater force upon the stone.
> Mine upraised was snatched with her away.
> Untouched about me now my carvings lie.
> I know not what to do. I am alone,
> Unless the great Artificer will show the way.

While Vittoria Colonna was still alive, Michelangelo did a crucifix for her which is quite astounding in its resolution of conflict, because the attempt is made to depict at once the crucifixion and the resurrection. A modern interpreter will not, however, have it so. He points to the statement of an intimate of Michelangelo that this crucifix seems to be saying, "Eli, Eli, My God why hast thou forsaken me?" But this friend records only his own interpretation, not that of the artist. The drawing must, therefore, speak for itself.

There is no look of desolation in this face. The reply may be that Michelangelo tended to mute the physical expressions of spiritual pain. Witness the *Pietà* at the Vatican with its gentle brooding melancholy. True, but in this drawing, the expression of physical pain does appear in the face of the cherub at our left, and much more so than in the face of Christ, who seems rather to be saying, "Father, into thy hands I commit my spirit!" The head is upright. The eyes are open. The mouth is open as if for speech, not sagging in death. The arms are starkly horizontal, the body vertical. There are no lacerations from the flagellation. The wound on the side is betokened only by the gesture of the cherub. This is the *bel corpo ignudo* of Michelangelo's David. Here we have a combination of the crucifixion and the resurrection, of the derelict upon the cross and the victor over sin and death. Beauty, suffering, and triumph are brought together. Gothic aspiration and classical form are combined.

But the artist could never quite achieve the triumph to which he aspired, for his brush and chisel could never encompass that which eye hath not seen but which yet enters into the heart of man. Let not the artist, however, despise his role, nor cease to suggest that which in its fullness is reserved for the vision of God.

Figure 218. Michelangelo Buonarroti. The Crucifixion (for Vittoria Colonna)

22
CHRIST BEYOND HISTORY

Up to now we have examined Christ's image in art according to episodes in the life of the historical Jesus. His deeds and sayings have all along served the Church by way of example and instruction. His passion gave the assurance of the forgiveness of sins and his resurrection, confidence in eternal life. The roles of Christ beyond history were suggested by symbols and titles. He was the Good Shepherd, the light of the world, the vine, the Lamb of God, the bridegroom of the Church and of believers, the second person of the Trinity, the King of Kings, the Judge at the great assize, and the sustainer of the universe. So real was the presence of Christ in the life of the Christian community that Athanasius, in arguing for the resurrection, did not turn to history but asked, "Is he a dead Christ who is working such transformations in the lives of believers?"

Some of these symbols have already received a measure of treatment. We have noticed the depictions of the Good Shepherd in the frescoes of the catacombs and on the early sarcophagi. Christ as the light of the world can scarcely be portrayed. We have noticed the attempt by Holman Hunt, which appealed to an earlier generation but appears to ours to be too contrived. The artists Correggio and Rembrandt do better to suggest the theme by showing a circle of faces all equally lighted by the babe in the manger. The other symbols and titles call for fuller treatment.

23
VINE

ANTICIPATING HIS ARREST, Jesus com-
forted and strengthened his disciples by saying, "I am the vine.
You are the branches. As the branch cannot bear fruit of itself unless
it abides in the vine, neither can you unless you abide in me." The
theme is delicately handled in a Netherlandish devotional manual
of 1325. The vine terminates in the cross and is topped by the
pelican, the bird symbolizing the resurrection. On our right the
winged lion, the sign of St. Mark, appears to be restoring a youth,
as the lion was reputed to be able to resuscitate a cub three days
dead. The other birds appear to be only decorative.

This chaste treatment of the theme was replaced in the late
Middle Ages, especially in Germany, by a lapse into the gross
primitivism of imbibing the spirit by drinking the blood. The point
of departure was the text in Isaiah 63:2-3. "Why are your garments
red, your clothes as if you had trodden the winepress? I have trod
the winepress alone." The prophet was treading out the grapes,
Christ was depicted as the grapes being trodden. Even the baby
Jesus was to be squashed and the adult pressed that his blood might
spurt through a bunghole into the chalice.

Figure 219. Christ the Vine

Figure 220. Baby Jesus in the winepress

Figure 221. The threaded posts

I find this treatment utterly repulsive not only on aesthetic grounds—Jesus squashed to a bloody pulp—but because, as in the case of the eucharistic crucifix, we have here the error that the soul is in the blood (Genesis 9:4), as if it were not in every portion of the anatomy. The reply may be that this is an emasculated metaphor, like loving from the heart or showing courage from the guts. It is granted that errors may become innocuous, provided that the primitive is not revived.

Such a lapse is not so offensive in the late Middle Ages as in our own day of scientific physiology. There is a revival. A German church in 1947 was decorated with a depiction fit for half a millennium ago. And the Guild of St. Mark of the Episcopal Church, as late as 1950, issued a devotional manual in which the crucifix is flanked by two threaded posts. Even a recent writer in *Liturgical Arts* offers a portrayal as ghastly and crude as anything in the Middle Ages.

24
LAMB

NTIL THE SIXTH CENTURY there was considerable reluctance to portray Christ on the cross. The Gnostic sects could not believe that the God-man could have suffered in the flesh. In some of the apocryphal gospels, Jesus is represented as having had no real body at all. His feet left no imprints. Or again, he did have a body, but not like ours, for on the cross he experienced no pain. Another version was that on the cross his body and divine spirit parted company and the body cried out, "My divine power, my divine power why have you forsaken me?" The most extreme solution was that someone else was on the cross. As late as 1400, a Gnostic sect in Ethiopia showed the two thieves on crosses. The cross of Christ was empty, though on the sides were the soldiers with spear and sponge. The bulk of the Christians rejected such views, yet they, too, found it easier to envisage the incarnation in the manger than on the cross. The debates of the fifth century as to the natures of Christ led to such an insistence on the genuineness of the human nature, that portrayals of the crucified came into vogue.

Until then however, the suffering of the Savior was signified by the symbol of the lamb. For this usage, abundant warrant was

Figure 224. Gnostic crucifixion

Figure 225. Adoration of the Lamb

195

Figure 226. The Lamb on the cross

Figure 227. Eucharistic Lamb

to be found in the New Testament. John the Baptist pointed to Jesus and said, "Behold the Lamb of God who takes away the sins of the world" (John 1:29 and 36). In the Book of Revelation, the Lord is called *the Lamb* ten times more frequently than *the Christ.* The Lamb holds the Book of Life. The Lamb is the conqueror, the judge, the bridegroom. In adoration of the Lamb, the four living creatures and the four and twenty elders fall down and sing a new song (Revelation 5:8–10). A magnificent depiction of this scene in a medieval manuscript is shown here. Another illustration goes even so far as to portray the crucifix with a lamb's head (Figure 226). The initial letter and Figure 227 are from Luther's Bible.

The Protestant reformers saw no reason to reject imagery present in the New Testament. While they clearly went beyond the New Testament in retaining the eucharistic theme of the blood streaming from the breast into the chalice, the reformers strongly objected to treating the Lamb as an amulet. There were little wax lambs, called *Agnus Dei,* able to forestall all ills, just as Bibles have been carried over the heart to deflect bullets. One of Luther's students wrote to his mother: "*Liebe Mutter,* I am grateful to you for sending me the little wax *Agnus Dei* to protect me against being shot, cut, and from falling. But honestly, it won't do me any good. I cannot set my faith on it, because God's Word teaches me to trust only in Jesus Christ. I am sending it back. We'll try it out on this letter and see whether it is protected from tampering. I hope you won't give the wax lamb to my brother."

Better to pray with W. E. Orchard: "Is this Thy form, a bleeding Lamb? . . . O Man upon Thy cross, we cannot turn back now; for our weakness, pain, and need are more than we can bear; Thy sorrow stays our feet. Thy suffering stirs our hearts. Thy sacrifice has saved our souls. O Lamb of God, we come."

25
BRIDEGROOM

RIDAL IMAGERY IN THE LATE
Middle Ages appealed especially to celibates. The depiction took
two forms, stemming from two Biblical passages. The first is
Ephesians 5:32, in which marriage is declared to be a great mystery,
indicative of the relationship of Christ and the Church. The other
passage is Revelation 19:7, which celebrates the marriage of the
Lamb. Hence the pictures show sometimes Christ, the man, and
sometimes Christ, the Lamb. Figure 228 depicts Christ and the
Church in affectionate poses. A cycle elaborates a verse in the

Figure 228. Christ and the Church in affectionate poses

Song of Solomon (5:7), where the bride laments that while seeking the groom, she was maltreated by the watchmen of the city. This is illustrated in Figure 229. The bride and groom appear at the top. Both are crowned. He gives her a ring. Then a robber assails her, knocks off her crown, and locks her in a cell. The groom with the shield of the cross disposes of the assailant and restores the crown. Figure 230 shows the Lamb giving the ring. The wedding banquet is depicted below. The man on our left at the table appears to be cutting a chunk from a loaf. Only the figure to the far right is paying any attention to the bride.

These and other similar portrayals come from the twelfth century. This was a period, as we noted, of amazing contrasts. None was more striking than that of attitudes toward sexual relations. We have, on the one hand, the cult of romantic love. It was a religion of a sort. The lover was uplifted by imbibing the excellence of the beloved. Romantic love was not matrimonial. Queen Eleanor said that love was impossible in marriage because the wife was the property of the husband and the lady went with the lands. Love might be addressed to a married woman, but to one only. No promiscuity! In such a relationship, love was often incapable of fulfillment, and the poetry of romance is full of languishing, though languishing was not the ideal.

Over and against this glorification of the erotic we have, in the Manichees, a complete rejection. They would eat nothing connected with sex and fortunately did not know that fish and plants have sex. The Church, at this time, imposed celibacy on the secular clergy, and tracts proliferated in denigration of women and marriage. The sexual urge found its sublimation partly in the cult of the Virgin—

Figure 229. Cycle of the Bride and Bridegroom

Figure 230. The Lamb gives the ring

the unattainable beloved—and partly through the image of the heavenly bridegroom to whom the Church and the individual believer could be spiritually married.

An influential figure in this regard during the twelfth century was St. Bernard. He dreamed that the crucifix, though still held by a nail through the feet, detached itself from the cross and bent over to embrace him. More influential than the picture of this dream was a meditation by the saint on the first verse of the Song of Solomon which begins, "Oh that you would kiss me with the kisses of your mouth!" Bernard elaborates her feeling: "I shall not be content," she says,

> unless he kisses me with the kisses of his mouth. I am grateful for a kiss of the feet. I am grateful for the kiss of the hand. But if he loves me, may he kiss me with the kisses of his mouth. I am not ungrateful. I have received, I admit, favors beyond my desert, but they are below my desire. I am carried away by my desires. It is not reason by which I am impelled. Accuse me not of boldness. This is the fruit of ardent love. Modesty indeed retreats. But love drives away all modesty. I know that the honor given to a king should be tempered with judgment, but a violent love does not know the meaning of judgment. It does not hearken to counsels, is not held back by modesty. It obeys not reason. I pray, I plead, I implore that he kiss me with the kiss of his lips (Sermon IX).

And all this is treated as an allegory of love for Christ.

26
SECOND PERSON OF THE TRINITY

F ALL THE DOCTRINES of the Church, none is more difficult and dangerous to portray than the Trinity, for fear of suggesting that Christians worship three gods. The three rabbits may be the least dangerous of all. The doctrine itself is very rich as a formula, giving expression alike to the simplicity and the complexity of God. He is one, He is three; Father, Son, and Spirit. Here we have monism and pluralism. The three are one beyond all time, for there never "was when the Son was not." The Father could not be timelessly father if the Son were not timelessly the son; the same for the Spirit. Their relationship is both static and dynamic, unchangeable, yet always becoming, seeing that the Father begets the Son, the Spirit proceeds from the Father, and, according to the western Church, also from the Son. Eternity and time are included. Though the relationship was before time, yet at a point in time the Word became flesh. How could a concept so varied, so rich, be given graphic representation? How to reduce such a nexus to a formula? One and three mathematically are not

Figure 231. The Trinity as three identical men

Figure 232. The Trinity as three men distinguished

Figure 233. The Trinity as one body, three heads

Figure 234. The Trinity as one head, three faces

equal. If they are to be made equal, poetry must be invoked, not arithmetic.

Consequently, graphic depiction of the Trinity arose but slowly and was always fraught with misgiving. One reason was that to show three beings gave a handle to the charge of the Jews and the Muslims that the Christians worshipped three gods. A deeper reason was the assumed impossibility of depicting God without blasphemy, except by a hand extending from above. Not until the eighth century do we find an extant example of a full, direct portrayal of the Three in one. (We do have a description of a portrayal in a church in the late fourth century, but the church is not extant.) To be sure, the separate parts appear. The depictions of the baptism have the hand above, the dove as the Spirit, and the Son receiving the rite. But there is no suggestion that the three are conjoined. Then there are symbolic representations: in a circle three birds, three men holding each other's heels, three rabbits sharing their ears.

The era of extensive direct depiction begins in the twelfth century. Is this another phase of that materialization of religion which we noted in this period with respect to the crucifixion and the resurrection? The Trinity is shown sometimes as three un-differentiated old men. Other depictions distinguish the Father wearing a papal tiara, the Son carrying the cross, and the Spirit with the dove perched on the halo. The unity is the more emphasized when one body has three heads, or one head has three faces. Another

Figure 235. The toes of God the Father

type combined the crucifixion and the Trinity. God the Father holds the cross bearing the body of the Son, and the dove of the Spirit links the beard of the Father with the halo of the Son, while the toes of God the Father Almighty stick out at the bottom. In 1626, Pope Urban VIII ordered all such pictures burned.

The development described above took place in the West. The East obviated the difficulties by using only symbolic representation, as the three holy persons were identified with the three angels entertained by Abraham. The noblest and the best known handling of this theme is the icon of the Russian artist Rublev, executed in 1425. His mode of treatment passed muster with a Russian synod meeting in Moscow in 1667 which, condemning the type prevalent in the West, decreed: "To represent the God of Sabaoth on icons with a gray beard, with His only Son in His lap, and a dove between them, is exceedingly absurd and unseemly, since no one has seen God the Father. For the Father has no flesh, and it was not in the flesh that the Son was born from the Father before all ages. . . . This birth, before all ages, of the only begotten Son from the Father cannot be understood by the mind, and must not be and cannot be represented on icons."

Figure 236. Andrei Rublev.
The three angels signifying the Trinity

Rublev went back to the verse in Genesis 18:1–2: "And the Lord appeared to Abraham by the oaks of Mamre, as he sat at the door of his tent in the heat of the day. He lifted up his eyes and looked, and behold, three men stood in front of him." Rublev's icon shows the oak of Mamre in the background and Abraham's house (not tent). The unity of the Trinity is symbolized by a circular composition. The circumference of the circle passes through a point above the head of the central angel and below the feet of the other two. The figures are nearly identical, but nevertheless individual. The Father is on the left. His colors are of an indefinite hue, since He is ineffable. The Son incarnate is given the traditional colors with the purple chiton tunic and the blue cloak. The Spirit is clad in green symbolizing the vitality of youth. A historian of the icons comments: "This icon with its inexhaustible equilibrium of composition, majestically calm figures of the Angels, light, joyous summer colors, could be the creation only of a man who had stilled in his soul all agitation and doubt and was illumined by the light of the knowledge of God."

27
PANTOCRATOR

VER THE RAINBOW IN MAJESTY
enthroned sits the Lord of all that is. He was called the "Pantocrator" in the East, "Christ in Majesty" in the West. Both styles
influenced each other, for the boundaries were never sharp. In the
sixth century, Ravenna, Italy, was the western capital of the eastern
empire. Then, too, Sicily and southern Italy had long had Greek
settlements, and some of the finest examples of Byzantine art are
to be found in Sicily.

The portrayal of Christ "seated at the right hand of God the
Father," as the creed said, was slow in emerging. In the East, one

Figure 237. Coin of Justinian II. Young Christ

Figure 238. Coin of Justinian II. Older Christ

factor was political. Constantine contributed some of the ideas, though he was not interested in the art. Only the monogram of Christ and not the head of Christ appeared on his helmet. Yet he gave an impetus to the concept of Christ as the ruler of the universe. Constantine believed in one God, one Lord, one faith, one baptism, and one Constantine. He had abdicated as God, but he was God's lieutenant and Christ's servant. To elevate the suzerain was to exalt the vassal, though if the suzerain were unduly exalted, the vassal might be inconveniently overshadowed. If his subjects preferred to swear before an image of Christ rather than of the emperor, one solution would be to remove the image of Christ. This, as we have seen, was among the motives for iconoclasm.

Another way out was to exalt the suzerain so high that he would be remote from human affairs. In the seventh century, the emperor Justinian II made a hesitant move in that direction. On his coins are two forms of the image of Christ. In the one he is young, with only fuzz on the chin and short hair.(Fig. 237.) This is the human Christ, the one who may meddle with the affairs of men. "The king of all rulers," says the inscription. On the other coin, though the inscription is the same, Christ is much older with long beard and hair. He is of the type which, after the Iconoclastic controversy, came back as the Pantocrator. In both styles the right hand was raised in blessing, the left held a book.

Figure 239. Christ on a throne

207

Figure 240. Christ on the circle of the earth

Figure 241. Christ on the rainbow

The elevation of the Pantocrator advanced by stages. The emperor was at first willing to have the Christ's image next to his own, especially during the Persian wars when Christ was believed to head his armies. There was no objection to having Christ seated on a throne. But when subjects preferred to make contracts by oath before Christ and the Persians had been subdued, Christ was depicted as sitting more remotely on the circle of the earth. The final stage was to seat him on a rainbow.

But let it not be supposed that the celebration of Christ as the Lord of the entire cosmos was merely a political move. The great drive for the images came from below—from peasants and especially women and monks. Here are selected lines from their poems and hymns marked by loftiness of conception and intensity of devotion:

How as a beloved son shall I nourish Thee who nourishest all?
How shall I bind Thee who art the bond of the universe?
Oh Logos God, who wast in the beginning with God,
Seeing that our nature was at the outset corrupted,
Transfuse Thy power, watch over our being.
In a second communion free us from passions.
Oh Thou who holdest and sustainest all that is
By the might of Thine omnipotent hand,
Oh immutable Logos of God,
Support and uphold all that give Thee praise,
Through the mediation of her that bore Thee,
Mother of God.
Thou Son of Him that begat without beginning,
Thou Lord become flesh through the Virgin,
Reveal Thyself to us and illumine our darkness.
Oh God, Pantocrator, Thou only unbounded,
Dwell Thou in me through unspeakable mercy.
Thou threefold Sun shine from on high.
Make me wise by Thy mercy.
Lord of all, triune Pantocrator,
Grant to Thy servants power with Thy Love, Thy faith,
That we may laud Thee, Thou lover of men, for ever and for ever.

Figure 242. Pantocrator

28
JUDGE

ISMISSING CHRIST BY ELEVATION
above the rainbow did not remove him from human affairs. The
creed says, "He sitteth on the right hand of God the Father almighty,
whence he shall come to judge the quick and the dead." The Lord of
the cosmos is the judge at the last assize. He is the keeper of the
Doomsday Book and will point out to some the sins they had not
recognized and commend others for the good deeds of which they
were not aware.

The picture of Christ the judge was congenial in the West
during the centuries of continuing barbarian invasions. Some
day, these robbers would receive retribution. The theme was
popular on the tympana of the Romanesque cathedrals. The
tympanum is the triangular or semicircular space above the portal.
It called for an elevated figure beneath the peak and lesser figures
grouped around. The judgment scene with Christ in the center,
admirably filled the space.

Figure 243 shows an example from the twelfth century cathedral at Autun in France. The key sufficiently explains the figures.

Figure 243. Tympanum at Autun

Figure 243 A. Diagram of tympanum at Autun

Note, however, that at the bottom in the center is an angel separating the damned at the right from the saved on the left. Among the saved, there is a pilgrim with the shell of Compostella on his coat. At the end on the right is one who looks as if he were striking a musical instrument. Let's hope he could have some fun in hell. Here is the key: *A*, Christ; *B*, the sun; *C*, the moon; *D* four times, angels upholding the mandorla (the oval in which Christ is set); *E*, Mary; *F* four times, angels blowing horns; *G*, possibly Enoch and Elijah; *H*, Peter; *I*, the Archangel Michael weighing souls; *J*, Satan doing the same; *K*, Angel, separating saved and damned; *L*, the damned; *M*, the saved; *N*, devils; *O*, angel boosting a soul into paradise; and *P*, gate of hell.

Figure 244. Hands extended to show the wounds

Figure 245. The Judge and the honeycomb

Figure 246. Vested angel of Judgment

Depictions of the wrath to come became too oppressive as the invasions receded. Attenuations were introduced. One was the assurance of intercession with the wrathful Son, by the compassionate mother. In our initial letter, Mary and John the Baptist are interceding with Christ on behalf of two little unbaptized babies already half-way down toward hell. At the same time, Christ the Judge was shown, not with his hands extended to separate the sheep and the goats, but upraised to display the wounds. (Figure 244.) A curious softening of terror appears in a judgment scene with a honeycomb at the bottom. The explanation is found in the words of St. Bernard: "Christ is my bee. He comes not to sting, but to bring me honey."

In the East, one wonders whether the viewer might not derive a certain confort from seeing the angels of the judgment vested in the robes of the Orthodox Church. In the late fifteenth century we have woodcuts in which mercy and wrath were evenly balanced. In Figure 247, a sword, signifying wrath, protrudes from one ear of Christ, and from the other the lily of mercy. But let it not be thought that terror was dispelled. We have a woodcut from close to Luther's day in which there is no lily, rather two swords. Below, a figure, probably Peter, is carrying a soul under his arm into Paradise. A devil has lassoed the foot and is bracing himself against Peter's rump to get more leverage to pull the soul over to hell. This was the sort of picture that threw Luther into a panic until he learned that the judge upon the rainbow was also the derelict upon the cross.

Figure 247. The Lily and the sword

Figure 248. Two swords

213

EPILOGUE

After surveying this vast range of the depictions of Christ, one is ever the more impressed by his universality. Every age and every clime has found in him that which has spoken to its condition. The point can be as easily illustrated from the literary as from the artistic tradition. A generation ago, a number of studies of Christ appeared with the most divergent emphases. There was Ernst Renan, who presented the idyllic, poetic Jesus:

> Often he went into a boat and taught his hearers crowded upon the shore. Sometimes, he sat down upon the hills which border the lake, where the air is so pure and the horizon so luminous. The faithful flock went also, cheerful wayfarers, receiving the inspiration of the Master in their first flower. . . . His preaching was sweet and gentle, full of nature and of the perfume of the field. He loved flowers, and he took from them his most charming lessons. The birds of heaven, the sea, the mountains, the play of children, were used by turns in his teachings.

To write these words, Renan had gone to the Holy Land with his adored sister Henrietta. While there, both were stricken by fever, and he awoke alone. His Jesus is Henrietta.

Bouck White, in *The Call of the Carpenter*, portrayed a Jesus seething with indignation against the exploitation of the poor by Rome, by the tax gatherers, and the money changers. He himself had been arrested when he sought to appear in the Riverside Church in New York City with a plea to the congregation to set up a commission to investigate the Ludlow massacre in copper mines controlled largely by Rockefeller.

Bruce Barton, in the advertising field, pictured Jesus as the supreme advertiser, who went into the market place and said striking things. He would have been successful in national advertising.

Mazumbra of India set forth the contemplative Christ, the incarnation of the cosmic spirit of life, while Kagawa, who dedicated himself to the slums of Kobe, exhibited the Christ who went about doing good.

They were all right. What they depicted was true, but distorted because partial. And to a degree they were misleading, because to make Christ just like one of ourselves is to obscure his greatness. Yet, one is reminded of what happened when the Turks took Constantinople and plastered over the mosaics of Christ. With the centuries, the plaster has cracked and the image of Christ shows through.

Nevertheless not all of the portrayals of Christ are even partially correct. To show him riding at the head of a crusading host and wading up to the fetlocks of his horse in the blood of the infidels simply will not do. These are perversions, and the extremes of diversity make one wonder whether Jesus is only a myth of man's creating, a manikin, which we, like the soldiers at the crucifixion, dress in our own clothes. The laborer will give him overalls, the advertiser a gabardine, the socialite a tuxedo, the priest a cassock, the soldier a uniform, the mystic the robe of an oriental sage. To his very disciples Jesus said, "Whom say ye that I am?" How much more pertinently may the same question be addressed to us at this far remove. Can we know?

Our only recourse is the record of the early Church. Jesus certainly stands at the head of a movement which shook the world. Yet he has not left a line. We have only the sayings and the deeds reported by those who had known him and the interpretation of Paul who had not known him in the flesh. Perhaps he can help us most because we are in his situation. Yet the New Testament does not entirely relieve us of our difficulty because there are different slants even here. The discourses of Jesus in John's gospel do not sound like the pithy sayings of the Sermon on the Mount.

At the same time there does emerge a figure with definite traits. Jesus is a reproving Christ. He deflated the pompous, punctured the proud, berated the exploiters, exposed the hypocrites, expelled the racketeers, put probing questions to the rich young ruler, and even by silence shamed the wrongdoer. The medieval monk was right in feeling that the eyes of the crucifix were ever upon him, searching the inmost recesses of his heart, discovering his secret sins, and causing him to fall upon his knees in shame and contrition.

Jesus is at the same time the comforting Christ. "Come unto me all ye that labor and are heavy laden." "My peace I give unto you." He relieved men of intolerable burdens, forgave their sins, had compassion on the multitude, wept over Jerusalem, and promised paradise to a dying thief beside him on a cross. In Jesus we find hope, confidence, and cheer.

Again, he is a redeeming Christ. The early Church based its very life upon the experience of redemption. The first Christians believed that Christ had introduced a new historical era. Old things had passed away. The old Adam had been superseded by the new, the covenant of tables of stone by the covenant of hearts of flesh. The Christian himself had become a new creature. The early Church father Origen, writing in the third century, already could say in his day that no philosopher of antiquity, no general of Greece or Rome had ever exercised such power over the wills of men as had the crucified Galilean.

Finally we must remember that Jesus is a suffering and a conquering Christ. No religion senses evil so profoundly as Christianity. None other has dared to take as its symbol an instrument of cruel execution, a cross. But this is not the final word. The cross, in the earliest depiction, is surmounted by the laurel wreath awarded to the victor in the games. The cross and the crown, tragedy and triumph, are drawn together by him who was "despised and rejected of men," yet to whom "every knee should bow."

ILLUSTRATIONS

GENERAL SOURCES

Works several times cited in the list of sources for illustrations:

Frere-Cook, Gervis, *Art and Architecture of Christianity* (Cleveland, Ohio, 1972).

Garrucci, Raffaele, *Storia della Arte Cristiana*, 6 vol. (1872–81).

Hind, Arthur M., *Introduction to a History of Woodcut* (London, 1935).

Kehrer, Hugo, *Die hl. drei Könige in Literatur und Kunst*, II (Leipzig, 1909).

Lehrs, Max, *Late Gothic Engravings of Germany and the Netherlands* (New York, 1969).

Newton, Eric and Neill, William, *2000 Years of Christian Art*. (Harper & Row, New York, 1966.)

Schiller, Gertrud, *Ikonographie der christlichen Kunst*. To date three volumes (Gutersloh, 1966–   ). The first two volumes are translated into English: Iconography of Christian Art (New York Graphic Society, 1971–   ). This book has the most valuable coverage. In addition to an explanatory text each volume has from 600–700 illustrations.

Schrade, Hubert, *Ikonographie der christlichen Kunst*. I. Die Auferstehung (Berlin, 1932).

Schramm, Albert, *Die Bilderschmuck der Frühdrucke*, 23 vols. (1920–43).

Takenaka, Masao. A work in Japanese on modern Japanese Christian Art, Shogensa, 45 Hinouecho, Kita-ku, Osaka, Japan.

Thoby, Paul, *Le Crucifix* (Nantes, 1959).

Wilpert, Joseph, *Roma Sotterranea* II (1903). Die römische Mosaiken (Freiburgi B., 1971).

SOURCES FOR ILLUSTRATIONS

Figure 1.   Derick Baegert. Luke Paints the Virgin and Child. Münster, Landesmuseum. From *Wallraf-Richartz-Jahrbuch*, X, p. 159.

Figure 2.   Martin Schongauer, Veronica's Napkin. Lehrs No. 369.

Figure 3.   The Good Shepherd (beardless, long hair). Drawn from *Encyclopedia of World Art*, III, p.1 304.

Figure 4.   The Good Shepherd (bearded, cropped hair). Drawn from Volbach, W. F., *Arte Paleocristiana* (1958).

Figure 5.   Earliest Virgin and Child. Catacomb Priscilla (1st half 2nd century). Wilpert, Joseph, *Roma Sotterranea*, II, Tav. 22.

Figure 6.   Virgin and Child (4th century). Drawn from Wilpert, Tav. 207. Catacomb Maius.

Figure 7.   The standardized portrayal of Christ. (Mid. 4th century). Drawn from Wilpert, Tav. 203.

Figure 8.   Celtic crucifix. The St. Gall Gospels. Reproduced in Allen, John Romilly, *Christian Symbolism in Great Britain and Ireland*, (London, 1887), fig. 36.

Figure 9.   Ichthys (fish) and Cross. Drawn from Cabrol, Fernand, *Dictionnaire d'Archéologie Chrétienne* VII, 2, p. 2078, No. 6112.

Figure 10.   Christian seal. Drawn from Garrucci VI, 477, No. 3.

Figure 11.   The Phoenix symbol. Drawn from Wulff, Oskar, *Altchristliche und Byzantinische Kunst* (Berlin, 1914), pl. 180.

Figures 12–13.   Symbols on Christian sarcophagi. Garrucci V, 374, No. 4; 307, No. 2.

Figure 14.   Cartoon against the Iconoclasts crucifying Christ afresh by giving vinegar to his image. MS Chludov (9th century), reproduced in Grabar, André, *Iconoclasme Byzantin* (Paris, 1957), pl. 143, Cf. p. 199.

Figure 15.   Holman Hunt. Christ as the Light of the World. Oxford, Keble College (1854). Reproduced in Schöne, Wolfgang, *Gottesbild im Abendlande* (1957), No. 67.

Figure 16.   Wilhelm Leib. Worshippers at prayer. *Ibid.*, No. 80.

Figure 17.   The flight into Egypt. Drawn from Tissot, J. James, *The Life of Our Saviour Jesus Christ*, I (New York, 1899), p. 32.

Figure 18.   John Everett Millais. Jesus in the workshop. (1850). Tate Gallery, London.

Figure 19.   Holman Hunt. Jesus the carpenter. Reproduced in Ward, W. H., *Year* (n.d.), p. 33.

Figure 20.   Rembrandt van Rijn. The boy Jesus in the Temple. Wilken v. Alten, "Rembrandt Zeichnungen," *Die Kunstbücher des Volkes* XLV (1947), No. 57.

Figure 21.   Decree of Augustus and journey to Bethlehem. Welfenschatz, Berlin, Staatl. Museum, Kunstgewerbe Museum, (Stiftung Preussischer Kulturbesitz). Drawn from Schiller I, 140.

Figure 22.   Jan Metsys. Rejection at the inn. Koninklijk Museum voor Schone Kunsten, Antwerp.

Figure 23.   No room in a Chinese inn. Society for the Propagation of Christian Knowledge, *Life of Christ by Chinese Artists* (1939).

Figure 24.   Ralph Coleman, A gentle refusal. Coleman, Ralph, *The Way, the Truth and the Life*, (1958), p. 49.

Figure 25.   James Reid, A brutal refusal. Reid, James, *Life of Christ in Woodcuts* (1930).

Figure 26.   Ox and ass without Mary and Joseph. Drawn from a Roman sarcophagus (ca. 333) reproduced in Schiller, I, 146.

Figure 27.   Mary recumbent: ox and ass tussling. Detail drawn from an illumination of 1290, Baltimore Waters Art Gallery, MS 759, reproduced in the *New Catholic Encyclopedia*, V, p. 4.

Figure 28.   Joseph cooking. Hind I, p. 98, fig. 39 (1410).

Figure 29.   Maid and midwife. Drawn from mosaic Cappela Palatina, Palermo, 1143. Schiller I, 159.

Figure 30.   Joseph lights a fire. Detail drawn from Conrad von Soest (1403–11) reproduced in Landolt, Hanspetter, *German Painting of the Late Middle Ages* (Skira, 1968).

Figure 31.   Joseph dries the diapers. Drawn from the reproduction in the *Encyclopedia of World Art* VI pl. 370.

Figure 32.   The tender touch. Stone relief, Chartres (ca. 1240). Reproduced *Ibid.*, pl. 344.

Figure 33.   The sparkling babe. The Master E.S., Lehrs, No. 130.

Figure 34.   Gerrit van Honthorst. The Light of the World. 1622, Cologne. Reproduced in *Propylaen Kunstgeschichte* IX, Abb. 184.

Figure 35.   Crèche. From the Metropolitan Museum.

Figure 36.   David Chituku. African nativity. Lehmann, *Die Kunst* 27.

Figure 37. A. D. Thomas. Indian nativity. *Ibid.,* 60.

Figure 38. Ki-Chang Kim. Korean nativity. Lehmann, *Christian Art,* 234.

Figure 39. Multitude of the Heavenly Host. Reichenau School, Codex Egberti (ca. 980). Trier Stadtbibliothek Codex 24, Schiller I, 167.

Figure 40. Winged Ethiopian ascetic. Drawing of an illumination in an early 18th century Ethiopic Prayer Book in the Spencer Collection of the New York Public Library.

Figure 41. Dante Gabriel Rossetti. Wingless Gabriel, from the Annunciation (1850). Tate Gallery, London.

Figure 42. "Electric spark." Boeckler, Albert, *Deutsche Buchmalerei Vorgotischer Zeit* (1952). München Bayerische Staatsbibliothek, Cod. Lat. 4452.

Figure 43. Shepherd as piping Pan. *Luttrell Psalter,* ed. George Miller (London, 1932), p. 28.

Figure 44. Peasant shepherds. Schramm XVI, 332.

Figure 45. Wajan Turun. Indonesian shepherds. Lehmann, *Christian Art,* 202.

Figure 46. Marcus Topno. Indian shepherds, Lehmann, *Die Kunst,* 70.

Figure 47. Babe in the manger and Child on the knee. Drawn from Kehrer Abb. 63. From stone relief, Notre Dame, Paris (ca. 1320).

Figure 48. The Child grasps the gifts. Ivory Abbey S. Denis (1339), in the Louvre. Kehrer p. 188, Abb. 222.

Figure 49. Varied numbers of the Wise Men. Two Wise Men: Kehrer, p. 1: Three: Garrucci V, p. 398, No. 4; Four: Wilpert, Tav. 116.

Figure 50. Ravenna mosaic. Volbach, W. F., *Arte Paleocristiana,* (1958), 181.

Figure 51. The Three Kings. See Fig. 43 for source.

Figure 52. Geoffrey Tory. Black Caspar (Paris, 1525). *Encyclopedia of World Art,* VI, pl. 408.

Figure 53. The angel pushes the star. Master E.S., Kehrer, p. 78, Abb. 65.

Figure 54. Jesus is the star. Schramm XXI, 55.

Figure 55. Theodora's robe. Detail drawn from André Grabar, *The Golden Age of Justinian* (New York, 1967), pl. 158.

Figure 56. Return by boat (ca. 1210). Bruchsaler Handschrift, Grossh. Hobibliothek, S. Peter I, Karlsruhe. Kehrer Abb. 170.

Figure 57. Frank's casket. British Museum.

Figure 58. Gentile da Fabriano. Italian Magi. Uffizi Gallery Florence. Reproduced in McGraw Hill, *Dictionary of Art* II, p. 484.

Figure 59. AghaBehzad. Modern Persian depiction. Lehmann, *Christian Art,* 207.

Figure 60. American Indian treatment. Lehmann, *Die Kunst,* 175.

Figure 61. Japanese version. Lehmann, *Christian Art,* 230.

Figure 62. Adoration of the Zulu Wise Men. Frere-Cook, Gervis, *Art and Architecture,* p. 240.

Figure 63. 10th century depiction. Fifth-century depiction. West Roman ivory relief, Berlin Staatliches, Museum Inv. Nr. 2719. Schiller I, 302.

Figure 64. 10th century depiction. Boeckler, Albert, *Das goldene Evangelienbuch Heinrich III* (Berlin, 1933), 171. Gotha Landesbibliothek MSi. 19. Ev. Echternach.

Figure 65. 13th century depiction. Stone relief, Notre Dame, Paris. Terrasse, Charles, *La Cathedrale*

Figure 66. (1946), p. 106.

Figure 67. Martin Schongauer. The bent palm. *Stiche und Radierungen,* Janitsch und Lichtwark (Berlin, 1885) I, 3.

Figure 68. Lucas Cranach the Elder. Rest on the flight. *Lucas Cranach Sammlung,* ed. F. Lippmann (Berlin, 1895), No. 33.

Figure 69. Mary teaches Jesus to walk. *Biblia Pauperum* (ca. 1460), Graphische Gesellschaft, *Veröffentlichungen* II (Berlin, 1906).

Figure 70. Joseph gives Jesus a "piggyback" ride. Detail drawn from Wilpert, Joseph, *Die römischen Mosaiken* (1917), p. 771, fig. 342. Capella Palatina.

Figure 71. Boy Jesus in the Temple. Schramm IV, 172.

Figure 72. Jesus helps in the shop. Schramm XIX, 170.

Figure 73. Jesus helps with the washing: Schramm XXI, 438.

Figure 74. Detail from Diego Rivera's "Vaccination." Drawn from a mural in the Detroit Institute of Arts. Detroit, Michigan, 1932. Reproduced in the *New Catholic Encyclopedia,* p. 526.

Figure 75. Catacomb depiction of the baptism. Drawn from Schiller I, 366.

Figure 76. Traditional depiction of the baptism (9th century). Schiller I, 366.

Figure 77. Jordan personified. Byzantine mosaic (early 11th century), Katholikon of the Monastery of *Hosias Lukas* near Delphi, Schiller I, 362.

Figure 78. Baptistry at Dura Europos. Kraeling, Karl, *The Christian Building.* Drawings adapted.

Figure 79A. El Greco. Baptism. Schiller I, 387.

Figure 79B. El Greco. Resurrection. Ipser, Karl, *El Greco,* (Braunschweig, Berlin, 1960), p. 223.

Figure 80. Loaves and fishes. Schramm XXI, 440.

Figure 81. Karl Thylmann. Healing of the leper. Horn, Curt, *Das Christusbild unserer Zeit* (Berlin, 1929), p. 31.

Figure 82. The Gaderene swine. Drawn from the illuminated Gospel of Otto III (Holy Roman Emperor 983–1002).

Figure 83. Sadao Watanabe. Japanese treatment. From Takanaka, Masao, *Creation and Redemption through Japanese Art* (1966).

Figure 84. The Prodigal in the far country. School of Lucas Cranach. Reproduced in *Wallraf-Richartz-Jahrbuch* XXVIII (1966), p. 245, No. 254.

Figure 85. Albrecht Dürer. Contrition. Tietze, H. and F. *Kritische Verzeichnis der Werke Albrecht Dürers* I, (Leipzig, 1937), No. 49.

Figure 86. Peter Opitz. Repentance. *Das Münster,* XII, p. 192.

Figure 87. Lucas Ch'en. Return. Lehmann, *Die Kunst* 114.

Figure 88. Van Gogh. The Good Samaritan. *Encyclopedia of World Art* V, pl. 120. Otterlo Neth. Museum.

Figure 89. Thomas Derrick. Modern treatment. Derrick, Thomas, *The Prodigal Son* (1931), p. 7.

Figure 90. Triumphal Entry, Western style (A.D. 340). Schiller II, 31.

Figure 91. Triumphal Entry, Eastern style. Mosaic (12th century) from Palatine Chapel. Hutton, Edward. *The Life of Christ in Old Italian Masters* (New York, 1935).

Figure 92. The Ass and the colt. Esternacher School

(1020–30). Schiller II, 42.

Figure 93.   The *Palmesel*. Metropolitan Museum.

Figure 94.   Anointing with oil and tears. Besançon Psalter (ca. 1260) Schiller II, 27.

Figure 95.   Chiding the apostles (*Apli*) and Judas. Reichenauer Egberti Codex (ca. 980), Schiller II, 29.

Figure 96.   Strasbourg's depiction. From *Passio der Vier Evangelisten,* printed by Johann Grundlinger, Strasbourg (1506). Bibliothèque Municipale of Strasbourg.

Figure 97.   Christ driving out the money changers. *Passional Christi und Antichristi* (Facsimile Berlin, 1885).

Figure 98.   Pope raking in the gulden. *Ibid.*

Figure 99.   Rembrandt van Rijn. Retreat of the money changers. Bredius, A., *Paintings of Rembrandt* II, 2, p. 532.

Figure 100A.   Peter's protest. Detail drawn from mosaic, *Hosios Loukas* (ca. 1000), Schiller II, 125.

Figure 100B.   Peter tested. Detail drawn from MS Monte Cassino (ca. 1100), Schiller II, 126.

Figure 100C.   Gesture of shoe removal. Detail drawn from an ivory in Rome (1071–5). Schiller II. 130.

Figure 100D.   Christ's humility. Detail drawn from *Cotton Psalter,* London. Schiller II, 134.

Figure 100E.   Christ's example. Schramm XVIII, 304.

Figure 101.   Sadao Watanabe. Japanese treatment. See Fig. 83.

Figure 102.   St. Louis IX of France washing the feet of beggars (14th century). Hermann, Julius, *Die westeuropaische Handschriften 2, Englische, Französiche* (1936), pl. XXI, No. 5.

Figure 103.   Agapé with baskets of loaves. Catacomb of Priscilla, Rome. Drawn from Grabar, pl. 8.

Figure 104.   Agapé with mixture of water and wine. Drawn from Laurent, *L'Art Chretien.*

Figure 105.   Ethiopian Lord's Supper. Drawn from *Jahrbücher für Antike und Christentum* IV (1961), Taf. 3.

Figure 106.   Richard West. American Indian Lord's Supper. Lehmann, *Christian Art,* 76.

Figure 107.   School of Giotto. Christ as priest. Schiller II, 105.

Figure 108.   Judas and the blackbird. *Stuttgart Psalter* (820–30). Stuttgart Württembergische Landesbibliothek, Codex 23, fol. 43n. Schiller II, 81.

Figure 109.   Dieric Bouts. Similar Netherlandish treatment. Panel (1464–67), College Church of St. Pièrre, Louvain, Belgium. Schöne, Wolfgang, *Dieric Bouts* (Berlin, 1938), Taf. 20.

Figure 110.   Leonardo da Vinci. The animated Lord's Supper. Touring Club Italiano, *Conosci l'Italia* VI, *L'Arte nel Rinascimento* (Milan, 1962), Taf. 101, No. 174.

Figure 111.   Tintoretto. The Supper in a tavern. Schiller II, 111.

Figure 112.   Albrecht Dürer. Lord's Supper (1510). Knappe, Karl-Adolf, *Dürer* (London, 1965), No. 184.

Figure 113.   Albrecht Dürer. Lord's Supper (1523). *Ibid.,* No. 367.

Figure 114.   Lucas Cranach the Younger (1515–86). Luther and companions at the Lord's Supper.

Figure 115.   Albrecht Dürer. Dürer as the Man of Sorrows. Waetzoldt, Wilhelm, *Dürer und seine Zeit* (Phaidon Press, 1935), No. 19.

Figure 116.   Hans Cranach (d. 1537). Cranach as Simon of Cyrene carrying the cross. *Antithesis Figurata Vitae Christi et Antichristi* (Wittenberg, J. Grüneberg, 1521) from a catalog of E. P. Goldschmidt prior to 1947.

Figure 117.   Lucas Cranach. John Frederick carries a cross from Max Geisberg, *Bilder-Katalog,* München, Hugo Schmidt Verlag, 1930.

Figure 118.   Michael Ell. Modern German version. Otto Dilschneider, *Formed Gospel* (Berlin, 1947), p. 79.

Figure 119.   Christ in Gethsemane. Lehrs, 36.

Figure 120.   Ethiopian depiction of the agony in the garden. *Evangeliarum of the Emperor Fasiladas* (1632–67). *Encyclopedia World Art* V, pl. 22.

Figure 121.   El Greco's treatment. Detail (ca. 1590). London National Gallery. *Encyclopedia of World Art* VI, pl. 452.

Figure 122.   Doré's engraving. Doré, Paul Gustave, *The Bible Illustrated* (New York, n.d.).

Figure 123.   James Reid. Woodcut. Reid, James, *Life of Christ in Woodcuts* (1930).

Figure 124.   Richard West. Christ as an American Indian. Lehmann, *Christian Art,* 78.

Figure 125.   Giotto di Bondoni. The Judas kiss. Arena Chapel. Padua (1305–7). Schiller II, 178.

Figure 126.   Gustav van Woestijne. Modern version of the Judas kiss (1937). Fine Arts Museum, Brussels. McGraw-Hill *Dictionary.*

Figure 127.   Peter severs the ear of Malchus. Stone relief, Nürnberg Cathedral (1250–60). Schiller II, 176.

Figure 128.   Judas hangs himself. Buchmalerei (820–30). *Stuttgart Psalter.* Schiller II, 164.

Figures 129–30.   Peter and the cock. Drawn from Schiller II, 163. *Pantokrator Psalter* (9th century), Byzantine.

Figure 131.   Peter and the servant girl. Drawn from Gospel. Palat. N.5, (end 11th century), Parma Bible Palatina. in *Art Bull.* XVII, p. 222, Fig. 34.

Figure 132.   A. D. Thomas, Indian treatment. Lehmann, *Die Kunst,* 119.

Figure 133.   Francisco José Goya. Peter's remorse. Zapater y Gomez, Don Francisco, *Collection de . . . Quadres de Goya* (Madrid, 1924), No. 215.

Figure 134.   Flagellation. Copy after Hans Hirtz, *Geisselung,* Veste Coburg. *Zeitschrift für Kunstwissenschaft* I (1947), No. 18.

Figure 135.   Crown of thorns. From Bonaventura, *Devote Meditazione,* Venice (1489–90). Hind, p. 475, fig. 233.

Figure 136.   Matthias Grünewald. Blindfolding. Glaser, Kurt, *Die Altdeutsche Malerei* (1924), p. 312, Abb. 212.

Figure 137.   *Arma Christi.* Buchmalerei (beginning 14th century). Schiller II, 655 and 656.

Figure 138.   Diadem of thorns. *Zeitschrift für Kunstwissenschaft* XII, p. 91, Abb. 18.

Figure 139.   Albrecht Dürer. Man of Sorrows. Schiller II, 726.

Figure 140.   Man of Sorrows from Luther's Bible. Schramm, Albert, *Luther und die Bibel* (Leipzig, 1923), No. 181.

Figure 141.   Caiaphas rends his garment. Schramm IV, Taf. 81, No. 551.

Figure 142.   Pilate's wife and Pilate washing his hands (15th century). Schiller II, 222.

Figure 143.   Dürer's depiction (16th century). Knappe, Karl Adolf, *Dürer* (London, 1965), No. 200.

Figure 144.   Ralph Coleman, Before Pilate (20th century).

Coleman, Ralph, *The Way, the Truth and the Life* (1958), pp. 106–7.

Figure 145. Barabbas chained. Drawn from Munoz, A., *Codex Purpureus Rossanensis* (ca. 575, Rome, 1907) Tav. XIV.

Figure 146. Jörg Ratgeb. Barabbas in prison. Stuttgart Staatsgalerie, reproduced in *Münchner Jahrbuch* III, 3/4, p. 192, fig. 1.

Figure 147. Rembrandt van Rijn. Barabbas on the balcony (1655). Winternitz, Emmanuel, "Rembrandt's Christ," *Oud Holland* LXXXIV (1969), 177–98.

Figure 148. Quentin Massys. The rabble on the balcony. *Burlington Magazine* LXXXIX, opp. p. 115.

Figure 149. Antonio Ciseri (1821–91), Pilate faces the mob. Galeria Nazionale d'Arte Moderna, Reproduced in *Year, Bible and Christianity*.

Figure 150. Hans Hirtz. Mary and John on the way to the cross. Karlsruhe Kunsthalle, reproduced in *Das Münster* IX, p. 386.

Figure 151. E. Koch. The collapse on the way to the cross. Woodcut from East Germany, reproduced in *Das Münster* II, p. 105.

Figure 152. Stecher. Erecting the cross. *Zeitschrift für Kunstwissenschaft* I, Abb. 10.

Figure 153. Christ mounts the cross. Italian (middle 14th century). Schiller II, 304.

Figure 154. The cross and the wreath. Sarcophagus, Lateran Museum (middle 4th century). Doerries, Hermann, *Konstantin der Grosse* (Stuttgart, 1958), pl. 12.

Figure 155. Earliest depiction of Christ on the cross. Dölger, Franz, *Die Fisch Denkmäler* (Münster i. W., 1927). Taf. 209, No. 13.

Figure 156. Crucifix (ca. 400). Ivory, British Museum. Schiller II, 323.

Figure 157. Crucifix (ca. 500). Drawn from the *Rabula Gospel* reproduced in Robert Browning, *Justinian and Theodora* (New York, 1971).

Figure 158. Crucifix with loin cloth at Rome. S. Sabina Door at Rome (A.D. 432). Schiller II, 326.

Figure 159. Villard de Honnecourt. The dead Christ on the cross (ca. 1250). Paris, Bibliothèque Nationale.

Figure 160. The single nail. *Das Münster* XII, p. 107.

Figure 161. Eucharistic crucifix. Lehrs 56.

Figure 162. Giovanni Bellini. Crucifix and pagan sacrifice. Painting entitled *Man of Sorrows*, National Gallery London.

Figure 163. From Gianlorenzo Bernini. "The Fountain Filled with Blood." An engraving entitled *Sangue di Cristo* in a work by Machese, *Unica Speranza* (Venice, 1691). Vatican Library. Reproduced in *Art Bulletin* LIV (1972). An engraving taken from the work by F. Spierre (1671). *Encyclopedia of World Art* XI, pl. 454.

Figure 164. The crucifix consoling St. Bernard. Drawn from Tiburtius Humpfner, *Ikonographie des hl Bernard von Clairvaux* (Augsburg, 1927), p. 24.

Figure 165. School of Giotto. "Weep not for me." Fresco (ca. 1325). Thoby, Paul, *Histoire du Crucifix* (1959), No. 274.

Figure 166. Christ comforted by Lady Poverty. *Bonaventura Gemelli's Umrisse zu Dante's Göttlicher Komödie*, ed. M. Jordan (Leipzig, 1879). Illustration for *Paradiso* XI, verses 70–72.

Figure 167. German crucifix with blood on the legs.

Colmar, Collection Mangold, 14th century. Source, Thoby, No. 313.

Figure 168. Hans Holbein. Christ of agony. Augsburg, Musee Maximilien. Thoby, No. 368.

Figure 169. Matthias Grünewald. Unutterable desolation. Isenheim Crucifixion (ca. 1509). From Newton and Neill, p. 169.

Figure 170. Mexican. Blood-reeking crown of thorns. Instituto National, *Mexico, Angustias de sus Cristos* (Cordoba 43, Mexico D.F., 1917), pl. 29.

Figure 171. Ignacio Zuloaga. Flagellation. Hispanic Society, New York. Reproduced in *Art Bulletin* VII, opp. p. 127, fig. 12.

Figure 172. Pablo Picasso. Christ the matador. *Toros y Toreros* (Abrams, New York, 1961).

Figure 173. Miracle of the diverted bull. Cossio, José Maria de, *Los Toros* II (Madrid, 1947), p. 229.

Figure 174. Pablo Picasso. Bones on the cross. Zervos, Christian, *Dessins de Pablo Picasso*, Cahiers d'Art, (Paris, 1949), No. 100.

Figure 175. The bull on the cross. Eisenstein, S. M., *Les Dessins Mexicans* (Sovietski Khoudojnik, Moscow, 1969), No. 72.

Figure 176. Detachable arms of the crucifix. Taubert, Gesine and Johannes, "Mittelalterliche Krucifixie mit Schwenkbaren Armen," *Deutscher Verein für Kunstwissenschaft* XXIII, 1, 1969.

Figure 177. Rembrandt van Rijn. Eli! Eli! Eli! (My God! My God!). *Rembrandt's Drawings and Etchings* for the Bible (United Church Press, 1969), No. 231.

Figure 178. William Blake. Darkness on the face of the land. Binjon, Laurence, *Drawings and Engravings of William Blake* (London, 1922), pl. 65, page 76 of Blake's *Jerusalem* (1808–18), British Museum.

Figure 179. George Rouault. Infinite sadness. Engraving in the *Miserere* Series (1922–27). From Newton and Neill.

Figure 180. Marc Chagall. The eternal Jew. His *White Crucifixion* (1938). Reproduced in the *New Catholic Encyclopedia* IV, p. 496, fig. 21.

Figure 181. Deposition from the cross with Joseph of Arimethea and Nicodemus. Boeckler, Albert, *Deutsche Buckmalerei* (reprint 1959), No. 27.

Figure 182. Ethiopian depiction. Frere-Cook, Gervis, *Art and Architecture* (1972), No. 29.

Figure 183. From Desvallière's deposition. Detail drawn from Paul Doncoeur, *Le Christ dans l'Art Francais* (Paris, 1939), p. 84.

Figure 184. W. de Silva. Ceylonese depiction. Lehmann, *Christian Art*, 100.

Figure 185. Hans Holbein. The dead Christ. *Holbein's Paintings* (Hyperion Press, 1938). Kunstmuseum, Basel.

Figure 186. 15th century pietà. Hind, p. 122, fig. 53.

Figure 187. "No comeliness." *Wallraf- Richartz Jahrbuch* XXIV, 1962, p. 117, Abb. 47.

Figure 188. Giovanni Bellini. Pietà. *Old Master Drawings*, No. 2 (Sept. 1926), pl. 58.

Figure 189. Michelangelo Buonarroti. The pensive Mary. Pietà, Rome, Vatican. *Encyclopedia of World Art* IX, pl. 526.

Figure 190. Rubbed-out pietà. Namban Art, *Christian Art in Japan*, by Tei Nashimura 1549-1639. Published by Kadansha, 3-19, Otowa, Bunkyo-Ku, Tokyo.

Figure 191. Jonah dancing above the waves. Schrade. Taf.

18. No. 74.

Figure 192. Ascension and resurrection. Ivory (ca. 400), British Museum. Schiller III, 12; also in *Wallraf-Richartz Jahrbuch* XXV, Abb. 27, p. 159.

Figure 193. Bartolomeo Schedoni. The three Marys (1614). Parma Galleria Nazionale. *Propylaen Kunstgeschichte* IX, after No. 38, description p. 134.

Figure 194. Knocking open the gate of Hades. Schiller III, 163.

Figure 195. Release of the spirits in prison. Schiller III, 167.

Figure 196. Albrecht Dürer. The release and the penitent thief. Schiller III, 95.

Figure 197. Trampling on the demon. Schiller III, 96.

Figure 198. Christ the crusader. From an English Apocalypse (14th century), reproduced in Anton Freitag, *Die Wege des Heils* (Salzburg, 1960), p. 54, No. 173.

Figure 199. The general resurrection. Ivory Cologne (ca. 1000). Schiller III, 174.

Figure 200. Earliest depiction of Christ stepping from the tomb. Reichenau Evangeliar (A.D. 1020). Schiller III, 187.

Figure 201. Meister Franke. A cautious emergence. Hamburg Kunsthalle. Schiller III, 223.

Figure 202. Peter Paul Rubens. A tumultuous emergence. Schiller III, 255.

Figure 203. The waltzing Christ. Detail drawn from Andrea Boscoli, Uffizi, Florence. Schrade, Taf. 42.

Figure 204. Wajan Turun. Resurrection as ascension in Indonesia. Lehmann, *Christian Art,* 203.

Figure 205. Matthias Grünewald. Resurrection at midnight. Schiller III, 238.

Figure 206. Through the closed door. Schrade, Taf. 5.

Figure 207. "Touch Me Not" (10th century). Evangeliar Otto III, Reichenau, München, Schiller III, 280.

Figure 208. Martin Schongauer. "Touch Me Not" (16th century). Lehrs, 367.

Figure 209. Albrecht Dürer. The gardener. Knappe, Karl-Adolf, *Dürer* (Thames and Hudson, 1965).

Figure 210. Rembrandt van Rijn. Before dawn. His "Touch Me Not" reproduced in *Zeitschrift für Bildende Kunst* V, opp. 248.

Figure 211. Doubting Thomas (11th century). Evangeliar from St. Peter's Salzburg. Schiller III, 359.

Figure 212. Polidoro da Caravaggio. Doubting Thomas (1595). Potsdam, Schiller III, 369.

Figure 213. Polidoro da Caravaggio. His earlier Emmaus (ca. 1598). Newton and Neill, p. 194.

Figure 214. Polidoro da Caravaggio. His later Emmaus (1606). Milan, Pinacotta di Brera, 318.

Figure 215. Offer of a fish. From the so-called Prayer book of Hildegard of Bingen (ca. 1190). Bayerische Staatsbibliothek, München. Schiller III, 357.

Figure 216. Great commission. Pericopienbuch, Heinrich II, 1007 or 1012. München, Bayerische Staatsbibliothek. Schiller III, 391.

Figure 217. Michelangelo Buonarroti. Christ bursting from the tomb. Paris, Louvre. Schrade. Taf. 33, No. 134.

Figure 218. Michelangelo Buonarroti: *The Crucifixion* for Vittoria Colonna. British Museum. Reproduced in my *Women of the Reformation: Germany and Italy,* p. 215.

Figure 219. Christ the Vine. *Netherlandish Book of Devotion* (1325). Beineke Library of Yale University.

Figure 220. Baby Jesus in the winepress. Woodcut in *Psalter of the Blessed Virgin* (late 15th century). Thomas, A., *Darstellung Christi in der Kelter* (1936), Taf. 18, Abb. 34.

Figure 221. The threaded posts. (Executed in 1837). See Thomas *op. cit.* Taf. 21. Reproduced in *Pilgrim Path*, compiled by Frederick E. Mortimer (1950).

Figure 222. Max Lacher. Modern German depiction. *Das Münster* II (1947-48).

Figure 223. Roland P. Litzenburger. American revival. *Liturgical Arts* XXXV, (Nov. 1966), p. 111.

Figure 224. Gnostic crucifixion. Detail drawn from an illuminated Ethiopic Gospel Book (ca. 1400). *New Catholic Encyclopedia*, V, 591.

Figure 225. Adoration of the Lamb. *Codex Aureus of the Bayerische Staatsbibliothek* (Facsimile Hugo Schmid Verlag, 1921), Beinecke Library Yale University.

Figure 226. The Lamb on the cross. Hunt, J. Eric, *English and Welsh Crucifixes 690-1550*, (SPCK, London, 1956), p. 19, No. 8.

Figure 227. Eucharistic Lamb. Schramm, Albert, *Luther und die Bibel* (Leipzig, 1923), Taf. 70, p. 121.

Figure 228. Christ and the Church in affectionate poses. *Zeitschrift für Kunstwissenschaft* XIII, p. 171, Abb. 11-12.

Figure 229. Cycle of the Bride and the Bridegroom. *Lexikon der Christlichen Ikonographie*, drawn from Bräutigaam (Herder Freiburg, 1968).

Figure 230. The Lamb gives the ring. Bibliothèque Nationale, Paris, MS lat. 10474, fol. 39v. Reproduced in *Art Bulletin* LII, No. 13. Article by George Henderson.

Figure 231-234. Representations of the Trinity. From Adolphe Napoléon Didron, *Iconographie Chrétienne* (Paris, 1843) and Karl von Spiess, *Trinitätsdarstellungen mit dem Dreigesichte* (Vienna, 1914). Hackel, Alfred. *Die Trinität in der Kunst* (Berlin, 1931).

Figure 235. The toes of God the Father. *Der Landgrafen Psalter* (early 13th century), p. 171. Edited Karl Löfler, (Leipzig, 1925), preserved in the Württemburg Landesbibliothek.

Figure 236. Andrei Rublev. The three angels signifying the Trinity. Reproduced in *Art Bulletin* XII, 4 (Dec. 1930).

Figure 237. Coin of Justinian II. Young Christ. Grabar, André, *L'Iconoclasme Byzantin* (1957), No. 18.

Figure 238. Coin of Justinian II. Older Christ, *Ibid.,* No. 13.

Figure 239. Christ on a throne. Berger, Robert, *Die Darstellung des Thronenden Christus* (1926), p. 23, Abb. 10. Wechselberg Schlosskirche.

Figure 240. Christ on the circle of the earth. *Ibid.,* p. 61. Abb. 37. Miniature from the Gospel Book of the Emperor Lothair. Paris, Bibl. Nat.

Figure 241. Christ on the rainbow. *Ibid.,* p. 95, Abb. 57. Agia Sophia, Saloniki.

Figure 242. Pantocrator. Frere-Cook, Gervis, *Art and Architecture* (1972), pp. 32-33.

Figure 243. Tympanum at Autun. The west portal of the cathedral at Autun, France. *Zeitschrift für Kunstgeschichte* XXIX (1966), p. 267, No. 3.

Figure 243A. Diagram of tympanum at Autun. Drawing.

Figure 244. Hands extended to show the wounds. Berger (See Fig. 239), Abb. 100.

Figure 245. The Judge and the honeycomb. London,

Victoria and Albert Museum. *Zeitschrift für Kunstgeschichte* XXXII (1969, 1), p. 255.

Figure 246. Vested Angel of Judgment. A Byzantine vested angel, detail of a mosaic in the cathedral of Santa Maria, Torcello. *Art Bulletin* LIV (1972, 3), p. 266.

Figure 247. The Lily and the sword. Schedel, Hartmann, *Das Buch der Chronikon*, 1493. Beinecke Library, Yale University.

Figure 248. Two swords. Johannes Geffcken, *Der Bildercatechismus des fünfzehnten Jahrhunderts* (Leipzig, 1855).

Initial letters: The initial letters which open each chapter were assembled and drawn by the author. In many cases, a single letter is a composite of more than one reproduction. All the letters are based on a collection made by the author from various sources over a period of many years.

SELECTED BIBLIOGRAPHY

This bibliography contains works not listed or adequately covered in the list of illustrations.

Bahr, Hans Eckehard, *Theologische Untersuchungen der Kunst, Poiesis*, München, 1965.

Bailey, Albert Edward, *Art and Character* (Nashville, Tenn., 1938) *Arts and Religion* (New York, 1944).

Berliner, Rudolf, "The Freedom of Medieval Art," *Gazette des Beaux Arts* XXVIII (1945), p. 265f.

Bialostocki, Jan, "Iconography," *Dictionary of the History of Ideas II* (New York, 1973), pp. 224–41.

Encyclopedia of World Art XIV, "Tragedy and the Sublime," p. 267f.

Gilson, Etienne, *The Arts of the Beautiful* (New York, 1965). *Forms and Substances in the Arts* (New York, 1966).

Lehmann, Arno, *Die Kunst der Jungen Kirchen* (Berlin, 1955). *Christian Art in Africa and Asia* (St. Louis, 1966).

Mathews, Thomas, "Toward an Adequate Notion of Tradition in Christian Art", and Panniker, Raymond, "Letter to an Indian Christian Artist," Both in *Liturgical Arts* XXXII, 1 (1962–4), pages 9f and 43f.

Wind, Edgar, "Traditional Religion and Modern Man," *Art News* LII (1953), pp. 19–22, 60–63.

Schiller, Gertrud, *Ikonographie der christlichen Kunst*, To date three volumes (Gütersloh, 1966–). The first two volumes are translated into English: *Iconography of Christian Art* (New York Graphic Society, 1971–). This book has the most valuable coverage. In addition to an explanatory text each volume has from 600–700 illustrations.

Bailey, Albert Edward, *The Gospel in Art* (Boston, 1916). *Art Studies in the Life of Christ* (Chicago, 1917).

Bréhier, Louis, *L'Art Chrétien* (Paris, 1928).

Frere-Cook, Gervis, *Art and Architecture of Christianity* (Cleveland, 1972).

Kitzinger, Ernst, *Portraits of Christ* (Penguin, 1940).

Künstle, Karl, *Ikonographie der christlichen Kunst* 2 vols. (Freiburg i. 8, 1926–28).

Morey, Charles R., *Christian Art* (London, 1935).

Newton, Eric and Neill, William, *2000 Years of Christian Art* (Harper and Row, New York, 1966).

Réau, Louis, *Iconographie de l'Art chrétien* (Paris, 1955-59).

EARLY CHRISTIAN ART

Grabar, André, *Early Christian Art* (New York, 1968). *The Golden Age of Justinian* (New York, 1967).

Lowrie, Walter, *Art in the Early Church*. (New York, 1947).

Morey, Charles R., *Early Christian Art* (Princeton, 1942).

Rice, Talbot, *The Beginnings of Christian Art* (London, 1957).

Strzygoroski, Joseph, "The Origin of Christian Art," *Burlington Magazine*, XX (1911–12) 146f. Notes local differences in the East.

Volbach, Wolfgang Frederick, *Arte Paleocristiana* (Florence, 1958). *Early Christian Art* (New York, 1968).

MEDIEVAL CHRISTIAN ART

Grabar, André, *Early Medieval Painting* (New York, 1957), and other works.

Mâle, Émile, *Religious Art in the 12th to the 18th Century*, (New York, 1949).

Morey, Charles R., *Medieval Art* (New York, 1942).

NORTHERN RENAISSANCE

Benesch, Otto, *The Art of the Renaissance in Northern Europe* (Cambridge, Mass., 1947).

ICONOCLASM

Bevan, Edwyn R., *Holy Images* (London, 1940).

Campenhausen, Hans von, "Die Bilderfrage als theologisches Problem in der alten Kirche" in Wolfgang Schöne *Das Gottesbild im Abendlande*, (Witten, 1959).

Dobschütz, Ernst von, "Christusbilder," *Texte und Untersuchungen NF* III, XVIII (1898), lengthy account of the numbering of the commandments.

Encyclopedia Britannica, art. "Decalogue," brief account of the numbering of the commandments.

Eisenhöfer, Leo, "Die Siegelvorschläge des Clemens von Alexandrien und die älteste Literatur," *Jahrbuch für Antike und Christentum* III (1960), 51–70.

Grabar, André, *L'Iconoclasme Byzantin* (Paris, 1957).

BYZANTINE ART

Rice, David Talbot, *Byzantine Art* (London, 1935). *Byzantine Icons* (London, 1959).

Ouspensky, Leonid and Lossky, Vladimir, *The Meaning of the Icon* (Boston, 1952).

MODERN CHRISTIAN ART

Dillenberger, Jane, *Style and Content in Christian Art* (Nashville, Tenn., 1965). *Secular Art with Sacred Themes* (Nashville, Tenn., 1969).

Liturgical Arts, numerous articles, in particular: Muehlinberger, Richard Charles, "Sacred Art—a Critique of the Contemporary Situation," (XXVII, 1959), pp. 69–72. Bouler, André, "Meditation on Religious Art," (XXXV, 1966), 20–25. Mathews, Thomas, "The Future of Religious Art," (XXXV, 1966), 86–8.

Schöne, Wolfgang, *Das Gottesbild im Abendlande*, (Witten 1959) essays.

THE NATIVITY

Cornell, Hendrik, "Iconography of the Nativity of Christ, *Uppsala Universitets Arskrift* (1924, 1).

Dinkler-von Schubert, Erika, *Der Schrein der hl. Elisabeth zu Marburg,* (Marburg a.L., 1964). On the depiction of Joseph in the late Middle Ages: with a halo only, with the Jewish coned hat only, with both. pp. 14–20.

Meiss, Millar, "The Madonna of Humility," *Art Bulletin* XVIII (1936), p. 435f. On the reversal of the symbolism of the ox and the ass; for the patristic identification of the ox with the Jews, see Schiller, *op. cit.* I, p. 71. For the ox as the Christian Church, Erwin Panofsky, *Netherlandish Painting* (Cambridge, Mass., 1953), p. 278 and 470.

THE WISE MEN

Kehrer, Hugo, *Die hl. Drei Königen in Literatur und Kunst,* 2 vols. (Leipzig, 1908–9). Illustrations in volume II. That the black Wise Man was at first a buffoon II, 223.

THE LAST SUPPER:
Siren, Osvald, *Leonardo da Vinci* (New Haven, 1916) on the composition of Leonardo's Last Supper. Berenson, Bernhard, *Study and Criticism of Italian Art,* 3rd ser. (1916), pp. 21, 25. Comment on Leonardo.

THE CRUCIFIXION

Haussherr, Reiner, *Der Tote Christus am Kreuz* (Bonn, 1963). *Michelangelo's Krucifixus für Vittoria Colonna* (Opladen, 1971). Replete with valuable information, though I dissent as to this crucifix.

Gruber, Ernst, "Maiestas und Crucifix," *Art Bulletin* XX (1938), 268f.

Thoby, Paul, *Le Crucifix* (Nantes, 1959). *Art Bulletin,* LI (1969), p. 116. On the peak of the Devotion of the Holy Blood at Mantua in 1459.

THE RESURRECTION

Rademacher, Franz, "Zu den frühesten Darstellungen der Auferstehung Christi," *Zeitschrift für Kunstwissenschaft* XXVIII (1965), 195–218.

Schrade, Hubert, *Ikonographie der christlichen Kunst,* I. *Die Auferstehung* (Berlin, 1932f).

THE PANTOCRATOR

Berger, Robert, *Die Darstellung des thronenden Christus in der romanischen Kunst* (Reutlingen, 1926).

Capizzi, Carmelo, "Pantocrator" (in Greek letters), *Orientalia Christiana Analecta* CLXX (1964).

THE JUDGE

Grevot, Denis et Zarecki, George, *Gislebertus Sculpteur d'Autun* (Paris, 1960).

Sauerländer, Wilhelm, "Ueber die Komposition des Weltgerichts-Tympanum in Autun," *Zeitschrift für Kunstgeschichte* XXIX (1966).

THE YOUNGER CHURCHES

Note Lehmann and Takenaka, The SPCK etc. in the list of illustrations.

Lisbon *Exposicao de Arte Sacra Missionaria* (1951).

Fleming, Daniel, *Each with his own Brush* (New York, 1938).

Jobé, Joseph, *Ecce Homo* (Harper & Row, 1962).

THE ANGELS

Mendelsohn, Henriette, *Die Engel in der bildenden Kunst* (Berlin, 1907).

Vilette, J., *L'Ange dans l'Art d'Occident,* 12th and 13th centuries (Paris, 1940).

THE NIMBUS (HALO)

Collinet, Guerin, Marthe, *Histoire du Nimbe* (Paris, 1961).

76 77 10 9 8 7 6 5 4 3 2